90 DAYS
TO A
POSITIVE
MENTAL ATTITUDE

sound
wisdom.
Because Your Success Matters

Napoleon Hill's

90 DAYS

TO A

POSITIVE

MENTAL ATTITUDE

TRANSFORM YOUR OUTLOOK · TRANSFORM YOUR LIFE

DON M. GREEN

Executive Director and CEO,

THE NAPOLEON HILL FOUNDATION

Published and distributed by:

SOUND WISDOM
P.O. Box 310
Shippensburg, PA 17257-0310

717-530-2122

info@soundwisdom.com

www.soundwisdom.com

While efforts have been made to verify information contained in this publication, neither the author nor the publisher assumes any responsibility for errors, inaccuracies, or omissions. While this publication is chock-full of useful, practical information; it is not intended to be legal or accounting advice. All readers are advised to seek competent lawyers and accountants to follow laws and regulations that may apply to specific situations. The reader of this publication assumes responsibility for the use of the information. The author and publisher assume no responsibility or liability whatsoever on the behalf of the reader of this publication.

ISBN 13 TP: 978-1-64095-533-2

ISBN 13 eBook: 978-1-64095-534-9

For Worldwide Distribution, Printed in the U.S.A.

1 2 3 4 5 6 7 8 / 28 27 26 25 24

CONTENTS

INTRODUCTION

The effects of most motivational materials are usually temporary. After you attend a seminar or read a book you're fired up for a few days, but before long you're back in the same rut. This book is designed to help you make a lasting change in your life.

Its intent is to keep you permanently motivated by helping you form habits that will inevitably lead to happiness and success. The book provides an inspirational message each day for ninety days with each offering positive action steps that you can put into practice immediately.

This format will allow you to internalize the principles behind the messages so that you can apply them in your everyday life. The level of success you achieve in your life will depend upon the habits you form. If you do the right things, if you follow the proven principles of success that others have learned and applied, you will be successful.

It is inevitable.

Success seldom comes easily. It comes from forming the habit of doing the right things even when no one in the world expects you to succeed—except you. It is also true that big successes usually follow a series of small successes, each of which prepares you to reach higher and higher levels of performance. When you form the success habit, you know you will achieve your goal because you have taken the appropriate actions to ensure that you will.

Our intent is to provide you with the tools you need in an easy-to-use format with daily messages that can be readily understood and applied. You won't have to spend long hours each day studying a complex lesson, but you will have to make a commitment. Only you can decide that you are ready to change your life for the better. If you're ready, this book contains the secrets of outstanding achievement. Those secrets are yours for the taking.

To get the most from the book, read one article each day and attempt to apply the principles contained in it. Use the positive action steps at the end of each as a guide for the application of the principles. At the end of each week, review the positive action steps for the entire week to make sure you have them firmly implanted in your mind. Repeat this process until you have completed all ninety articles.

The final chapter contains a summary of all of the positive action steps and some suggestions for ensuring that you have internalized all the concepts and principles contained in the book. If you have completed the book and are still having difficulty putting some of the techniques into practice, re-read that section, and work on those principles until they, too, become a part of you.

If you find a passage that particularly appeals to you, or if the life of an achiever profiled in one of the articles is especially meaningful to you, underline or highlight that portion of the book. Return to it again and again when you need inspiration. As the great motivational writer Napoleon Hill said, "Motivation is like a fire. Unless you add fuel, it goes out."

Change isn't easy. We form bad habits the same way we form good ones—by repetition. If you really want to make a positive change in your life, you can. It is within your control, and yours alone. Only you can decide what kind of person you wish to be and what level of success you are capable of achieving.

The information you need to make the changes you desire are contained within these pages. The rest is up to you.

CHAPTER ONE

ATTITUDE IS EVERYTHING

With the proper attitude, everything is possible. Without it, nothing can be accomplished. If we believe we can win, we stand a good chance of doing just that. But if we believe we will lose, we already have.

DAY 1

TEN STEPS TO A POSITIVE MENTAL ATTITUDE

here seem to be two basic types of people in the world: those who cheerfully do the right thing, and those who, even when they do the right thing, do it grudgingly.

It doesn't require a Ph.D. to figure out that the person who does the right thing cheerfully will advance further in an organization, build a successful business, or succeed in whatever line of work he or she chooses. And it's simply a matter of attitude.

Insurance tycoon and motivational writer W. Clement Stone so believes in the importance of a positive mental attitude that he made it the linchpin of his philosophy of success. He defines a positive mental attitude as the appropriate attitude under any circumstance. It is not a naïve belief that if you look on the bright side, everything will work out. A positive mental attitude is also the absence of a negative mental attitude.

A positive attitude has the power to attract the good and the beautiful while a negative repels them, Stone says. He believes that a negative attitude not only ensures that you will not realize your true potential, it robs you of all that makes life worth living. He says, "A positive mental attitude combined with the selection of a specific goal is the starting point of all success."

"Your world will change whether or not you choose to change it," Stone says, "but, you do have the power to choose its direction. You can select your own targets."

"For centuries philosophers have been telling us: 'Know thyself.' But what we should really be teaching is not knowing and understanding yourself, but realizing that you have the potential within you to reach any goal in life that you desire as long as it doesn't violate the laws of God or the rights of your fellow man," Stone says.

"What the mind can conceive and believe," he maintains, "the mind of man can achieve with a positive mental attitude. We translate into physical reality the thoughts and attitudes we hold in our minds. We translate thoughts of poverty and failure into reality just as quickly as we do thoughts of riches and success. When our attitude toward ourselves is big and our attitude toward others is generous and merciful, we attract big, generous portions of success to ourselves!"

The right attitude toward your career and your life allows you to attack opportunity with zest and enthusiasm. You don't mind putting in a little overtime and extra effort required to do an outstanding job—instead of a mediocre one—because you know the rewards will come.

Although there are any number of ways of developing a positive mental attitude, here is a simple ten-step process developed by Napoleon Hill, author of the best-selling book, *Think and Grow Rich*, that provides great results:

1. Count your blessings daily and give thanks. You can't help but be more positive when you think of all you have to be positive about.

2. Keep your mind on the things you want and off the things you don't want. In other words, focus on the possible good in a situation instead of the possible bad.

3. Read, relate, and assimilate self-help materials. As Napoleon Hill pointed out: "Motivation is like a fire. Unless you add fuel, it goes out."

4. Use positive suggestion. Psychologists have long known that you can increase your chances of success in any given task if you stop and envision yourself succeeding beforehand.

5. Set and achieve a goal daily. It doesn't have to be a big goal. Even small accomplishments will do wonders for your self-confidence.

6. Be a "goodfinder," not a faultfinder. Looking for the good in others not only helps your attitude, it helps theirs as well.

7. Believe in yourself. When you believe in yourself, others will too. When you believe in yourself and others believe in you, anything is possible.

8. Share a part of what you have, a part that is good, with others. Nothing lightens the spirit more than helping others.

9. Help others develop a positive mental attitude. By doing so, you will be helping yourself.

10. Use your greatest power—the power of prayer.

At first, putting these principles to work may be difficult, but if you keep at it, maintaining a positive mental attitude will soon be automatic just as the rewards that come from a positive mental attitude are automatic.

A positive mental attitude can be the key to success and happiness not only in business ventures but in personal relationships, as well. In fact, there isn't a single facet of life that can't be improved with a positive mental attitude. Try it for yourself. I'm positive you'll enjoy the outcome.

—— POSITIVE ACTION STEPS ——

☞ Focus on solutions, not on problems.

☞ Associate with positive people. Avoid doomsayers.

☞ Engage in positive conversations. Avoid complaining.

DAY 2

PREPARING TO WIN

Someone once said that the desire to win isn't what makes a winner. The desire to prepare to win is what separates the winners from the losers.

Everyone desires to win, but preparing to win is the tough part, and I know from personal experience. A few years ago, when I went for my annual physical, my doctor told me that if I didn't lose twenty pounds and get into better shape, I was going to have some real problems. My blood pressure was already at the upper acceptable limit, and if I continued my sedentary lifestyle and questionable dietary habits, soon I would have clinical high blood pressure with all its associated risks, not to mention a future dependent on high blood pressure medication.

My doctor told me to go on diet, to exercise a minimum of a half hour a day three times a week, and come back in three months for a progress check.

After a few days of denial, I accepted the fact that I was going to have to change. This was difficult because I had never had a weight problem before. I had always sailed through physicals with flying colors. I never had to consider the fat content in foods. My four main food groups were cheeseburgers, French fries, hot dogs, and pizza.

I quickly decided I needed help. I read articles and books on healthy eating. I learned to read labels and cut fat. Then I set about the task of goal setting, budgeting time and resources, replacing bad habits with good ones, and developing personal discipline.

I decided that I would work out every day possible, not just three times a week. I would budget my time to include a workout. I would set definite measurable goals, and I would stick with the job until it was finished. It wasn't easy. In fact it was one of the toughest things I have ever done.

After the three months were up, my doctor was astounded. I had lost over nineteen pounds and my blood pressure was back to normal. And two years later, I'm in the best shape of my life.

I won this battle because I prepared to win by setting my mind on a definite goal and reading positive, motivational materials to reinforce my resolve.

As many people have pointed out, the human brain is like a computer—we get out of it what we put into it. So if we program our minds correctly, our success is ensured.

In programming our minds for success it's the garbage in, garbage out (GIGO) theory of programming. If we allow our human computer to be controlled by negative influences, the majority of our impulses will be negative. We will be controlled by negative thoughts, fear of failure, and the reluctance to risk anything new. However, if we eliminate negative thoughts one by one until they are all gone, we can begin replacing negative thoughts with their positive equivalent.

In the forest, it is impossible for most young saplings to flourish until older, larger trees have been removed. Sunlight cannot penetrate the leafy branches of mature trees to reach the forest floor and provide nourishment essential for the growth of new seedlings. But when a mature tree is removed, a miraculous thing occurs. In the space of a few weeks, the ground is covered with new growth. Seedlings sprout up everywhere, each reaching for the sun that was previously unavailable to them. So it is with negative attitudes.

When we have removed all the little negative thoughts until we have reached the core of our negativism, we are prepared for new positive growth. If we nurture and protect positive thoughts from the hostile environment that seeks to destroy them, they will gain the height and stature necessary to survive in a negative world.

Every living person has the potential to be positive, negative, or neutral, but potential is meaningless without action. Merely trying to remove negative thoughts will not make us positive. We must actively plant positive thoughts to keep negative ones from taking root again. Until we begin to do the things that are necessary to transform the way we think, we can never realize the great benefits of life that are ours for the taking.

One way to help develop a positive attitude is to study and absorb motivational and affirming messages daily. Set aside a half hour each day to study and think about success principles, your goals, and the next step you need to take to reach your goal. This helps clear away the deadwood and plant positive thoughts to take root throughout the day.

If you plant enough positive seeds, negative thoughts will have no room to grow.

── POSITIVE ACTION STEPS ──

☞ Set aside time each day to study success principles and to plan the next step in reaching your goal.

☞ Several times each day, stop and visualize yourself succeeding in your chosen endeavor.

☞ Seek out positive influences, experiences, and people. Avoid the negative.

DAY 3

HAPPINESS IS HARD WORK

There are two basic types of people: happy and unhappy. It seems that no matter how great things are, the unhappy types always find something to complain about. Happy people, on the other hand, always seem to bounce back quickly no matter how bad things get. So it would seem that one secret of happiness is not what happens to you, but how you choose to deal with it.

A happy, productive, fulfilled life comes from only one source: ourselves. The external environment can influence and affect our attitudes and emotions to some extent, but how we react to those outside influences is a matter of choice.

Since every individual is different in tastes, wants, desires, and needs, it may well be that happiness, like beauty, is in the eye of the beholder. We all crave different things, and as we grow and mature, we change, and so do the things that bring us pleasure. One thing is certain for each of us, however. Happiness is more than the mere absence of unhappiness.

As reported by Kathy Ulyott in *Chatelaine,* December 1990, Dr. Michael Fordyce, a psychology professor at Edison Community College in Fort Myers, Florida, found that most of us experience momentary happy moods, "but a truly happy individual manages to lead his or her life with a sense of emotional well-being and contentment, and overall feeling of satisfaction."

Dr. Fordyce also points out that simply avoiding things that make you unhappy does not make you happy; it only makes you neutral. Being happy is a positive, active state. It is not a passive condition in which you accept the happiness as though it were a gift. Creating the feeling of fulfillment, the euphoria that comes from achieving an important goal, or overcoming a difficult obstacle requires your active participation.

There is a great deal of truth in the old adage that busy people are happy people.

According to Dr. Fordyce, "Unhappy people waste a lot of time in idleness. Happy people keep busy and make sure they fit activities they enjoy into their daily schedule."

The emotions are not always subject to reason, but they always respond to action. Completing a job we've been avoiding, exercising—just about any activity that makes us feel productive and useful—makes us happier people.

It is also true that happiness generally involves trade-offs. Seldom can we do everything we wish; we simply don't have the time or stamina to fit everything in our lives that we would like. But like the song says, you can't always get what you want, but if you try sometime, you just might find you get what you need.

According to University of Chicago psychology professor Mihaly Csikszentmihalyi in Judy Woodburn's article, "What Makes Us Happy" in the January issue of *Special Report* magazine, "People are happiest when they are striving to achieve goals they have set for themselves. In short, happiness is often hard work."

When we are feeling overworked, this may be a difficult concept to embrace, but we wouldn't be permanently satisfied if life were one continuous day at the beach either.

After studying the subject for twenty-five years, Csikszentmihalyi concluded that the experiences we recall as the happiest of our lives occurred when we were so absorbed in what we were doing that we forgot about everything else. There is something inside ourselves that makes us feel unfulfilled unless we are challenged.

If work has become routine and boring, look for new ways to perform tedious tasks. Compete against yourself to improve your productivity. Use the time you save to learn something new and different. Develop outside interests. When you look forward to participating in a community event or learning to play a musical instrument, mundane chores become more bearable.

Happiness is never awarded to you; it must be earned. Don't resent others for what they have or dream about things you believe would make you happy. Happiness can only come from within, and you must create it.

Csikszentmihalyi's advice: "Pay attention to what you're doing in each moment. Enjoy your skills as you move from day to day, and become more in touch with your own potential. Don't let your mind be led from outside...realize that life is difficult but it's in your hands, and you can make it into what you want."

We can't all be CEO of the company, a famous rock star, or an Olympic runner. But in the diversity of our personalities and our capabilities is the very essence of what makes us alike and what makes us different. And although the objective for our lives and the goals we set for ourselves along the way may be vastly different, we all share one trait that is as old as life itself. We all want to improve, to be better at what we do. So it's only natural that we quickly become bored with doing the same thing over and over again.

—— POSITIVE ACTION STEPS ——

☞ Change your routine. Take a different way to work. Eat something different for lunch. Take a walk.

☞ Challenge yourself at work by doing more than the day before.

☞ Dive into your favorite hobby (watching TV doesn't count).

DAY 4

FEARS MASTERED

It was Asian philosopher Lao-Tzu who coined the phrase, "a journey of a thousand leagues begins with a single step." And that bit of wisdom applies equally to the process of overcoming failure and the fear of failure. We do it step by step.

The hardest part of any job is getting started, but almost nothing is as difficult as it first appears when we tackle it with enthusiasm and determination. Every time we try and fail, we become stronger, more capable people who will likely succeed next time. Our strength grows as we struggle.

Just as exercise strengthens muscles, overcoming obstacles teaches us to persist, to work harder and smarter, to eventually succeed. We become stronger, faster, and better at what we do, and the strengths we gain through trying and failing make us stronger in every other aspect of our lives as well.

When we eventually do succeed—and we will if we stay with it long enough—we develop newer and better ways of doing things. The techniques we develop through trial and error and trial and success teach us physical and mental shortcuts. Because we know how to do things better, we have more physical and mental energy to devote to more difficult tasks.

Obstacles to success make life far more interesting. Without them, there would be no challenges; without challenges life would become merely tedious.

There is more benefit in failure than there is in success, according to sales and marketing consultant David Driscoll. He suggests, in the April 1989 issue of *Sales and Marketing Management* magazine, that after a failed attempt, don't ask yourself: "What have I lost?" Instead, ask: "What have I gained?"

He points out that in sales there are far more opportunities to fail than there are to succeed. Good salespeople know that they are going to be rejected most of the time. They simply count each rejection as a "no" that they have gotten out of the way as they move toward a "yes."

"The more we fail, the more we succeed if we stay out there trying," Driscoll says. "It is a game based on the law of averages and percentages. However, we make it personal and upset the percentages."

From this day forward, ask: "Why did I fail?" Examine the answers carefully. Did you confirm any doubts and become more discouraged and not want to try again? Or did you realistically seek solutions, not excuses? By depersonalizing rejection, we can overcome our fears and more objectively evaluate our failures and learn from them.

Fear is often what keeps us from trying to succeed in the first place. Napoleon Hill said one of the best ways to overcome obstacles to success is to ask yourself bluntly: "What am I afraid of?"

He observed that once we confront our fears, we often find they turn out to be nothing more than mere shadows. Here are some of man's most basic fears and Hill's suggestions for overcoming them:

Fear of sickness. The human body is endowed with an ingenious system for automatic self-maintenance and repair. Why worry that it might get out of order? It's much better to marvel at how our bodies stay in proper working order in spite of the demands we place upon them.

Old age. Why fear it? Years are something to look forward to, not fear. We exchange youth for wisdom. Nothing is ever taken away from us without an equal or greater benefit being made available.

Fear of failure. If you really examine it, momentary failure is a blessing in disguise. Failure carries with it the seed of equivalent benefit—all we need to do is seek the cause of the failure, and we have gained valuable knowledge to better our effort on the next attempt.

Fear of death. All you need to do is recognize that death is a necessary part of the overall plan of the universe, provided by the Creator as a means of giving man a passageway to the higher plane of Eternity.

Fear of criticism. If you remember that you should be your own most severe critic, then what is there to fear in the criticism of others? Besides, such criticism may include constructive suggestions that will help you improve yourself.

Even physical pain, which many people fear unreasonably, plays a positive role in our lives. Pain is but a universal language by which even the most uneducated person knows when he or she is endangered by illness or injury.

As these examples illustrate, fear results mostly from ignorance. After all, man feared lighting until Franklin, Edison, and a few other rare individuals proved that lightning is simply a form of energy that could be harnessed for the benefit of humanity. To master your fears and find success, all you must do is open your mind through faith to the guidance of Divine Intelligence.

— POSITIVE ACTION STEPS —

☞ Talk to a trusted friend about your fears. A fresh viewpoint may be all you need to see that your fears aren't what they first seem.

☞ Visualize the worst-case scenario. Often you'll find you can live with the worst case and can even take comfort in the fact that the worst case almost never happens.

☞ Trust that things usually work out for the best. For instance, how many times have you heard about someone losing his job, only to discover a new position that makes him even happier?

DAY 5

LEARNING ENTHUSIASM

When you have a choice of people with whom to do business, whom do you prefer: a person who is enthusiastic about the job he or she is going to do for you, or someone who couldn't care less? Your answer tells you something about the importance of developing enthusiasm.

Fortunately, enthusiasm is something that can be learned—or perhaps re-learned. There is nothing more enthusiastic than a child. Children approach every day with a level of exuberance that makes many adults weary just to watch them. Each new discovery, however mundane it might appear to an adult, is exciting to a child.

The late Dr. Norman Vincent Peale, whose book *The Power of Positive Thinking* has sold millions of copies around the world, once reminded me that there is no such thing as a negative baby. "We learn to be negative the same way we learn anything else: by repetition," he said. "The only way to counter the world's negative influences is to eliminate negative thoughts and replace them with positive ones until there is no longer any room for negativism."

Positive thinking becomes a habit and a way of life when we choose to be positive and enthusiastic every day—when we choose to find joy in experiencing all of life's pleasures, however small they may be. A positive mental attitude powered by enthusiasm is a formidable force.

W. Clement Stone often says that the best way to be enthusiastic is to act enthusiastic. It's a concept that was dramatically impressed upon me recently.

Not long ago, as we were recording a radio show, I seemed to be having one of those days when nothing worked right. My mouth was out of sync with my brain, and I kept mispronouncing words. Then we started having technical difficulties. My annoyance level, both with myself and the situation, continued to escalate.

When the technical difficulties were finally resolved, about the last thing I wanted to do was try again. But I forced myself to talk with all the enthusiasm I could muster. Suddenly, a marvelous transformation took place. I actually began to feel enthusiastic. In the space of just a few seconds, I had gone from massive irritation to genuine enthusiasm.

I had practiced Mr. Stone's technique for years, but never before had I experienced such an instantaneous transformation—probably because circumstances had never required me to adapt so quickly before. The principle of enthusiasm works. If you doubt it, all you need to do is convince yourself to give it a try.

You'll find that enthusiasm is the engine that drives your success. Ralph Waldo Emerson said, "Every great and commanding movement in the annals of the world is the triumph of enthusiasm. Nothing great was ever achieved without it."

One of the surest ways to get others on your side is to approach every task with enthusiasm.

Even if you don't feel particularly enthusiastic, try to force yourself to act enthusiastically. Acting decisively and enthusiastically is the first step toward becoming decisive and enthusiastic.

Of course, the best way to generate enthusiasm is to do something you really like doing. If you hate your job, it will be very difficult to be enthusiastic about it. Conversely, it is virtually impossible to do something you like without being enthusiastic about it.

Long before the cosmetics company she founded became known all across America, Mary Kay Ash discovered when she was a young housewife and mother that she could sell things by the sheer force of her enthusiasm. Fascinated by a set of books on mothering that she desperately wanted, she almost cried when she found out how much they cost.

The saleswoman, sensing her interest and hoping for a sale, left the books with Ash over the weekend. When the saleswoman returned for the books, Ash told her that she was going to save until she could afford them, because they were the best books on the subject she had ever seen.

"When she saw how excited I was," Ash recalled later, "she said, 'I'll tell you what, Mary Kay, if you sell ten sets of books for me, I'll give you a set.'"

Ash thought this was a wonderful arrangement. She called her friends, neighbors, and the parents of the kids in her Sunday school class.

"I didn't even have the books to show them," she said. "All I had was my enthusiasm."

She sold the ten sets of books in a day and a half and so strongly believes in enthusiasm that she made the song "I've

Got That Mary Kay Enthusiasm" a part of the culture at Mary Kay cosmetics.

Enthusiasm sells. Have you ever seen a TV commercial for a product that didn't enthusiastically boast about the benefits of the product? If the company isn't excited about its product, how can you be expected to be enthusiastic enough to buy it? The same holds true in life. If you're not enthusiastic about what you're doing or selling, you can't expect others to be enthusiastic.

Your abilities, skills and resources are like a car, and enthusiasm is the fuel. Without fuel, your abilities, skills and resources won't take you very far.

—— POSITIVE ACTION STEPS ——

☞ To be enthusiastic, act enthusiastic.

☞ Enthusiasm is contagious. Associate
with enthusiastic people.

☞ If you're not enthusiastic about an idea or product,
you'll never get anyone else to be enthusiastic about it.

DAY 6

BUILDING ON SMALL SUCCESSES

Like many young men in the 1960s, George C. Fields experienced an epiphany in Vietnam. But unlike those who found only desperation and despair, Fields' road to Damascus was enlightening and uplifting.

After successfully avoiding military service for years with student deferments, he was drafted just months before his twenty-sixth birthday, the age when he would no longer be eligible for the draft.

"I spent a long time avoiding getting drafted," Fields recalled, "and from that experience I learned not to invest a lot of time and energy in avoiding things. The Army ended up being an extremely positive thing for me."

Fields also overcame his fear of heights in the Army. "I volunteered for airborne to force myself to face that fear," he said. "Airborne training separates those who are willing to face death from those who are not. They convince you that you are going to die when you step out of the plane, so in a sense every time you jump, you are choosing death before dishonor.

"My first jump wasn't nearly as bad as I imagined it would be," said Fields. "I went through the door and suddenly it was dead quiet. I looked up and saw my white chute against a beautiful blue sky, and all the other parachutes going down, and I was alive! I thought I was going to be dead, and instead I was floating down and everything was beautiful and fresh."

He also learned in the Army that he preferred to be around positive, enthusiastic people. "I was with an all-volunteer unit, and when you are with people who choose to do what they are doing, there is a much greater sense of enthusiasm and professionalism," he said.

Upon his discharge, Fields returned to his native Chicago. A political science major, he planned to write political philosophy when a friend persuaded him to interview for a job with Peterson Publishing Company as an advertising-space sales representative. The company offered him a position starting the following Monday. He declined in order to graduate, but returned to claim a job as soon as he completed college.

From Peterson, he went to Times Mirror Magazines where he quadrupled billings for *Popular Science*. Later at Knapp Communication's *Home* magazine he made *Adweek* magazine's Ten Hottest magazine list for two consecutive years.

When asked about his philosophy of success he says, "Negative people tend to focus on the misses instead of the hits. They forget that a great baseball player only hits .300; he misses seven out of ten times at bat. You have to think, 'Next time I'm going to get a hit!' and keep swinging. It's a dead certainty that if you think you are going to miss, you will, but if you keep doing the right things, eventually you will get those three hits out of ten that you need."

One technique for keeping our motivation up, to "keep in there swinging" when we'd rather give up, is to develop affirmations. Perhaps you remember the story of "the little engine that could."

By repeating over and over, "I think I can, I think I can," the train engine was able to make it over a great hill. That technique of self-affirmation can work for you too.

Over time, most goal-oriented people develop affirmations and self-motivators that they memorize and recall when they need a little encouragement They may be favorite quotations, catchphrases, or slogans that stick in your mind because they have a crisp, meaningful message. The important thing is to choose phrases that you find most appropriate and helpful to you.

Say them aloud several times each day until they become a part of you. Go to a private place (so other people won't think you've gone off your rocker), look at yourself in the mirror, and repeat—with all the enthusiasm you can muster—a single affirmation or self-motivation twenty times each morning and twenty times each evening for a week. It should then be firmly ingrained in your memory and can be recalled whenever you need it.

Although it's a good idea to develop your own affirmations, here are ten suggestions to get you started. Number one: Don't procrastinate; do it now! Number two: When the going gets tough, the tough get going. Number three: I am a good person. Number four: I deserve to be happy and successful. Number five: I can have anything I want if I am willing to work hard enough and smart enough to get it. Number six: He who hesitates is lost. Number seven: I am somebody! Number eight: I am what I think about most. Number nine: I am unique—a one-of-a-kind masterpiece. Number ten: All things are possible if you believe they are.

Sure, some people may ridicule the power of self-affirmation. Take for instance the reoccurring character of Stuart Smalley on NBCs *Saturday Night Live*, who is fond of saying, "I'm good

enough, I'm smart enough, and gosh darn it, people like me."
Sure he looks foolish when he says it, but affirmations are highly
personal things. They are not meant to be shared with others.
When used correctly, however, affirmations can replace negative
thoughts and reasons for failing.

It just makes sense that giving yourself a positive message to
dwell on is better than letting yourself wallow in a negative one.

—— POSITIVE ACTION STEPS ——

☞ Focus on the hits, not the misses. If you
believe you will fail, you already have.

☞ Develop a self-affirmation to help you concentrate
on an area of your life you would like to change.

☞ Repeat your affirmation aloud twenty times
each morning and each evening.

DAY 7

NEGATIVE THOUGHTS

It's an absolute certainty that you will never attract positive things if all of your thoughts are negative. Just as surely as a magnet attracts iron filings, your mind attracts the things you think about most.

One of the uncanny features of the mind is that it constantly seeks to turn into physical reality the things we think about most. Unfortunately, the subconscious mind—which concentrates on such thoughts twenty-four hours a day—can't distinguish between positive and negative thoughts. If you tell yourself something often enough, your subconscious will eventually come to believe it.

It doesn't matter if the information is truth or lies, fact or fiction, positive or negative thoughts. The mind is designed so that it constantly strives to attract the material equivalent of your most frequent and most prominent thoughts. It follows, then, that it is physically impossible for a negative mind to attract positive things. If you look for problems, you will find them.

It is possible, however, to overcome negative thinking, to replace pessimism with optimism. It is all a matter of conditioning. You can train your mind to think positive thoughts the same way you learn anything else—by repetition.

Dr. Norman Vincent Peale once told me a story that he used to drive home the point. Up on his farm in Duchess County, New

York, he had a dead tree that he feared might be blown over in a windstorm and damage his house. He called the landscapers who he thought would come out with a giant saw, cut down the tree, and haul it away. But they didn't do it that way at all. They started at the top, removing the branches one at a time until nothing was left but the trunk. Then they took the trunk down in sections until it, too, was gone.

He said, "That's how you deal with negative thinking. You remove negative thoughts one at a time until there are none left. Then you plant a new tree in their place. You water it, fertilize it, and nurture it with positive thoughts until it is strong and straight and so large that there isn't room for negative thoughts to grow."

If you make it a habit to stop negative thoughts every time they appear and replace them with their positive counterparts—if you replace "I can't" with "I can't fail"—you will soon find that your life has greatly improved.

You are what you think. W. Clement Stone and Napoleon Hill state it this way, "Whatever the mind can conceive and believe, it can achieve—with a positive mental attitude."

It is very likely that you will become what you think about most. If you are consumed by negative, destructive thoughts, you will be a sad and unhappy person. If you eliminate such thoughts and focus on positive things, you will become a happy, productive person.

It is a natural tendency of the mind to transform your thoughts into their physical equivalent. That's its job. Your mind is the central computer that tells you when to eat, sleep, and perform countless functions necessary for your survival and well-being. It is essential then that you control the input of your human computer. Otherwise it will behave exactly as its mechanical counterpart does: garbage in, garbage out.

Like most important aspects of your life, managing your thoughts and your expectations for your career, education, family, friendships, and health and fitness is not something decided upon and promptly dispensed with. It is a programming process that is time-consuming and often tedious and difficult. But it works.

Success in any endeavor begins with having a clear fix on what you would like to accomplish. Without an established destination, one direction is about as good as another. Goal setting puts you in charge of your life. You determine where you would like to be at any given time and you establish your own short-, medium-, and long-term goals to help you get there. Without fixed goals, you are likely to drift, driven by random external forces and events that have no real meaning or purpose for you.

In simplest terms, developing a plan for your life is similar to organizing a cross-country trip. Both require you to have a definite destination in mind if you are ever to have any hope of arriving there. Both have intermediate goals along the way that must be satisfied if you expect to reach your ultimate destination on schedule. A good plan will also have sufficient flexibility to accommodate detours and delays, and it will allow time for a side trip or two to check out interesting possibilities that arise unexpectedly.

Like any trip, however, the first and most important step is to determine your destination. When you know where you're headed, you will find all kinds of ways of getting there.

POSITIVE ACTION STEPS

☞ Set your goals by writing them down and
ranking them in importance to you.

☞ Devise a definite plan of action as to
how you will reach your goal.

☞ Keep in mind that—as with any trip—there may
be detours, setbacks, and some backtracking
before you reach your ultimate goal.

CHAPTER TWO

PERSONALITY PLUS

O ur personalities affect how we treat others, and ultimately how they treat us. Since we cannot achieve our goals by ourselves, personality becomes an important factor in our success. Week Two focuses on elements of a positive personality.

DAY 8

THE CHARACTER OF SUCCESS

The development of a positive personality begins with sincerity of purpose. Napoleon Hill related a number of anecdotes that illustrate the importance of being sincere in all you do. One involves Abraham Lincoln who was once told by a friend that his enemies were saying terrible things about him.

"I don't care what they say," Lincoln exclaimed, "so long as they're not telling the truth."

Sincerity of purpose made Lincoln immune to fear of criticism. The same trait helped him meet seemingly insurmountable problems growing out of the American Civil War.

Sincerity is a matter of motive. Therefore, it's something that others have a right to question before granting you their time, energy, or money.

Before embarking on a course of action, try testing your sincerity for yourself. Ask yourself: "Am I giving fair value in service or goods for the profit or wages I hope to make—or am I hoping to get something for nothing?"

Sincerity is one of the hardest things to prove to others. But you must be prepared and eager to do so.

Another Napoleon Hill anecdote illustrates how one person demonstrated her sincerity. Martha Berry founded a school many years ago for mountain boys and girls of north Georgia whose parents couldn't afford to pay for their schooling. To raise money to carry on her work, she sought and was granted an audience with Henry Ford. She asked for a modest donation, which Ford refused.

"Well then," said Miss Berry, "will you give us a bushel of peanuts?"

The novelty of the request so amused Ford that he gave her the money for the peanuts. Miss Berry showed her youngsters how to plant and replant the peanuts until their sales piled up $500—quite a substantial sum in those days. Then she took the money back to Ford and showed him how she had multiplied his small donation.

Ford was so impressed that he made her a gift of enough tractors and farm equipment to put her school farm on a self-supporting basis. Moreover, through the years he gave her more than $1 million for the beautiful stone buildings that now stand on the campus of the school Miss Berry founded.

"I couldn't help being impressed," Ford said, "with her sincerity and the marvelous way she applied it in behalf of the needy boys and girls."

Faced with adversity, Miss Berry learned that you can achieve your goals in life by demonstrating your sincere desire to make the lives of others easier or better through a product, service, or talent.

In fact, adversity can teach you many things. In his book *Think and Grow Rich*, Napoleon Hill wrote, "Adversity is good for us. The person who really ought to be pitied is the one who grows up with a 'silver spoon' in his mouth."

A person who grows up rich with no responsibilities will never be a strong competitor of the individual who had to fight hard for every foot of ground that he or she has covered. Hill points out, "It is not wealth that makes a person—it is character, persistence, and a strong determination to be of service to the world!"

Hill says that we might as well understand now that our real success will be measured and determined by the quantity and quality of service that we render the world. There is no guess-work, no luck or chance about this. It's according to nature's own laws. "You may be wealthy," says Hill, "but that isn't success. You may have a splendid education, but that isn't success either. You may have wealthy parents, but again, that isn't success."

The only real, permanent, and worthwhile success, according to Hill, "is represented by the character you are building."

He says that we are building some sort of character all the time. And that by devoting some of our time to self-improve-ment, like developing self-confidence and self-control, we are building a character that will be an asset in years to come.

Character is built slowly, step by step. Our every thought and every act goes into it. Character is the crystallization of the things we do, the words we speak, and the thoughts we think. "If you think about worthwhile things," says Hill, "you are pretty much apt to be a worthwhile person."

"You can be pretty much what you want to be if you will keep your mind on the one thing you want to be long enough. But that assumes that you also try your hardest, not just wish hardest."

Hill also explains that we should never complain if success does not come easily. If it did, we might not recognize it when it arrived!

He observed that "the world is waiting for men and women who are seeking the opportunity to render real service—the kind of service that lightens the burdens of our neighbors; the kind of service that makes the world a better place to live in; the kind of service that ninety-five out of a hundred people do not render because they do not understand it."

—— POSITIVE ACTION STEPS ——

☞ Make it your policy to always do more than you're asked to do.

☞ Always be sincere. And always be ready to prove you're sincere in your goals.

☞ On the job, find something that needs to be done...and do it.

DAY 9

A PLEASING PERSONALITY

Remember the old saying, "It's easier to catch flies with honey than with vinegar"? It's human nature to want to do business with those we like and avoid those we don't.

If competitive factors such as quality, service, price, and delivery are more or less equal, the deciding factor for most of us is to deal with people to whom we can relate. It is imperative that we develop a personality that others like.

The first essential is to develop character. It is unlikely that you can have a pleasing personality without the foundation of a sound, positive character. It is almost impossible for you not to telegraph your true character to those with whom you come in contact. That is why when you meet someone for the first time, you may have an intuitive feeling about that person, a like or dislike of that person without really knowing why.

The truth is, you can decide what kind of person you want to be. If you want to develop good and positive traits, emulate others you admire. Practice self-discipline to replace bad habits with good ones. Focus your mind on positive thoughts.

Always keep in mind that honesty and integrity are critical attributes of strong character. If you do not conduct yourself with integrity in all your dealings with others, you may succeed for a time, but your success will not endure. You need only to read the daily newspapers to see example after example of well-known, highly respected sports figures, stockbrokers, politicians, and others who have fallen into disgrace because of fatal character flaws.

Once you have built a solid foundation of good character, there are some specific things you can employ to make a good impression. First, be genuinely interested in others. Find their good qualities and praise them. Next, speak with force and conviction not only in meetings and public gatherings, but in private conversations as well. Dress for success according to your age, physical build, and type of work you do. And learn to give a good firm handshake. It sounds silly, but remember your impression the last time you received a cold-fish handshake? Next, be sure to talk about others' interests rather than your own.

If you're in business, it is especially important to develop a pleasing personality and strong character. After many years of working with both buyers and sellers of products and services, I am convinced that people will always find a way to do business with people they like. Regardless of the sophistication of the purchasing procedure or the expense of the product or service, we all have a natural tendency to do business with people we like. We make the decision emotionally, then work out the logical basis of the decision later, assuming, of course, that price, quality, and service between competitors are relatively constant.

Wayne Bilut, who was for many years the top printing salesman in the U.S., points out that salespeople often forget the old axiom in business, that a deal is not a good deal unless it is a good deal for everyone involved. Every person should benefit from the transaction.

Bilut says, "Salesmen often say 'gimme'—gimme an order or gimme a commission, but they don't respond in kind. They overlook the importance of investing in your customers." He says, "People what to be thanked somehow. You have to take action to let them know you appreciate them.

"Talk is cheap. Everyone says, 'Thanks for the order.' Really successful people spend time with their clients and customers; they let them know they are important. Buyers are human, and they need to know that the people they are dealing with are human. They need something besides simply exchanging paperwork; they need to feel good about life in general. People interaction makes the difference in building long-term relationships. Only a shortsighted salesperson tries to build a relationship on price alone."

Bilut always finds something in common with his customers, regardless of their diversity, something he says is not easy and "cannot be done in a sales call."

He says, "You have to get them away from the office—out to lunch or dinner or something—to find things in common. You need to understand their goals and career strategies so you can determine how to best help them and where you fit in."

To get to know each other well enough to share that kind of personal information demands that you spend time together, Bilut believes. But getting to know someone is the surest way that he or she will do business with you next time, not some stranger.

POSITIVE ACTION STEPS

☞ Learn to listen at least as much as you talk.

☞ Take a genuine interest and get to know your co-workers and customers.

☞ Ask questions. Most people like giving an opinion or talking about themselves.

DAY 10

LEND OTHERS A HELPING HAND

Some people think it's impossible to make money or achieve success without depriving others of it. Nothing could be further from the truth. In fact, it's almost impossible to amass a great fortune without helping others.

Napoleon Hill once pointed out that the truly great fortunes are amassed by men with the vision and courage to create a better service or product which, in turn, creates jobs, investment opportunities, sales, and wealth for large groups of people. However, the American system of economics is based—and rightly so—on competition. To be successful, you must learn to conduct yourself properly under competitive conditions between people, companies, products, and services. You must bring to this arena the same high standards of behavior that apply on the athletic field—things like good sportsmanship.

Good sportsmanship is a positive quality, not a passive one. Hill said instead of merely refraining from kicking others when they're down, we should give them a helping hand to get back on their feet. Your attitude should be the same in victory or defeat. It's in the moments of blackest adversity that the true sportsman shows the greatest courage and fighting spirit. And in the flush of victory, he shows the most solicitude for those he left behind in the race.

The mark of the true leader is not so much his greater courage, strength, or intelligence. It shows in his concern for those less favorably endowed by nature or circumstance. You can demonstrate your ability and right to lead others by exercising the extra measure of sportsmanship necessary to make their work a little easier and their existence a little more comfortable. When you smooth the road for others, you take the bumps out of it for yourself too.

Hill pointed to Art Linkletter as a good example of applying this principle. Besides his busy entertainment career, Art had his hands in literally scores of small business he helped others establish with his time, effort, advice, encouragement, and investments. As a result, he had interests in such diverse products and services as photo development, TV camera manufacturing, lead mines, a bowling alley, and a skating rink. The people he helped establish in these businesses recognized Art as a real leader.

As Hill said, "You can become the same kind of leader though dynamic sportsmanship. Don't just extend the hand of friendship to others. Make it a helping hand—and you'll help yourself."

Perhaps one of the surest ways to develop these qualities in yourself is to adopt and follow the Golden Rule. Briefly stated, it says: Do unto others as you would have them do unto you.

Back in 1920, Napoleon Hill published an article in his *Golden Rule* magazine pointing out the benefits of following this philosophy: "The Golden Rule Philosophy is the shining sun that forms the background for all other qualities on the ladder of success. Unless the Golden Rule lights the pathway over which you travel, you are apt to plunge headlong into pitfalls from which you can never escape."

Hill said that the Golden Rule makes dictators impossible, and it helps to produce Lincolns and Washingtons. It is the thing which leads individuals or nations into growth or decay, life, or death. The Golden Rule offers the only sure roadway to happiness, because it leads straight though the field of useful service in the interest of humanity. It is the thing which develops a cooperative spirit in man and causes him to submerge his selfish personal interests for the good of the group.

The Golden Rule acts as a barrier to all of man's tendencies toward the destructive use of the power which comes from developing the other qualities of an achiever. It is the thing which neutralizes the harm people can do with knowledge and power; it guides us to the intelligent, constructive use of those qualities which we develop from the use of the proven principles of success.

The Golden Rule is the torchlight by which we are guided toward those objectives in life that leave something of value to posterity, lightens the burdens of our fellow sojourners on earth, and helps us find the way to useful, constructive effort. Of course, merely reading or talking about the Golden Rule Philosophy will do you little good unless you develop its characteristics within yourself. You must work to achieve the promise that stands before you.

If you follow this philosophy, work will be pleasant and full of interest. It will seem more like play than work. Your rainbow's end is in sight, my friend, as Hill said, and the moment you master the principles of the Golden Rule Philosophy, you can pick up the bag of gold which is waiting there for the rightful owner to come along and claim it.

—— POSITIVE ACTION STEPS ——

☞ Be a good sport. Treat competitors as friends. You don't want to compete with enemies.

☞ Helping others doesn't have to take a huge investment of your time. Helping others is often as simple as making a call on their behalf or introducing them to the right person.

☞ Don't wait for others to ask for help; establish goodwill by looking for ways to help them now.

DAY 11

SIX STEPS TO BETTER RELATIONSHIPS

An old fly fisherman once told me that he likes to think of trout fishing as a metaphor for life. When you wade out into the mainstream, unless you have your feet firmly planted, you will just drift with the current.

It's true that we all need a grounding philosophy to keep us from drifting as the currents of life swirl about us. Having a well thought-out code of ethics that you abide by is also a wonderfully efficient way to deal with others. You never have to stop and ask yourself: Is what I'm doing legal? Is it moral? Is it ethical? If you've established a high set of standards that you will not allow yourself to go below, you won't have to waste time thinking about it. You will immediately know the answer.

I have a very simple code of ethics that I try to follow in my personal and professional relationships. It is:

I. I will be honest in all of my dealings with others.

2. I will not lie or attempt to deceive anyone.

3. I will not participate in any business relationship that is not fair to everyone involved.

4. If I must deliver bad news, I will do so with tact and understanding of the other person's point of view.

5.   I will attempt to follow the Golden Rule in all of my dealings with others.

6.   I will attempt to always do more than is expected of me.

I got the idea of writing down my code of ethics from ESPN hockey analyst Bill Clement. He framed his and hung it beside his desk. It's there for all the world to see, and it's there to remind him of what he's all about.

If you haven't developed a set of standards for yourself, you're welcome to borrow from mine. After all, I shamelessly stole most of it—some from Bill Clement and some from Socrates, Plato, Confucius, Jesus, and Mohammed. I don't think any of them would mind if you adopted their philosophy.

Once you have adopted your rigid set of standards, you will know how to conduct yourself in most any situation, and as a result you can cultivate better relationships with those around you.

At work cultivating good relationships not only makes your job more enjoyable, it can also make it more profitable. When morale is up, generally so is productivity. To improve relationships with your workers, simply treat them how you would wish to be treated. For example, Samuel Wheeler, a middle manager with a multinational company, was traveling on business when he got an emergency message to call his office in New York. Mary Clarke's mother had died in London, and the employee needed a $1,000 cash advance to go abroad and make funeral arrangements.

Wheeler knew it couldn't possibly be arranged in the two days before Mary had to leave, particularly if he wasn't there to steer the paperwork through the necessary bureaucratic channels. So he sent a sympathy note by Federal Express, along with his personal check for $1,000.

"Use the money to cover your expenses, take whatever time you need, and we will work out the details when you return," he wrote. Later, when Wheeler learned that company policy prohibited such cash advances, he simply made it a personal loan.

"Ours is a closely knit department," Wheeler said, "and Mary is very popular in the group. Although I wouldn't ordinarily make a personal loan to an employee, I felt that in this situation if I didn't do something, morale would have been seriously affected. I did what I had to do."

Family emergencies often blur the distinction that has traditionally existed between employees' personal and professional lives. Wheeler's method of handling Mary Clarke's case may have been unorthodox, but, as he said, he did what he felt he had to do.

It is not uncommon for companies to step in and provide assistance to employees with personal problems. For example, when Gene Mahaney, a longtime writer with the Chicago-based Leo Burnett advertising agency, died of a heart attack, a company representative went to Mahaney's house within a week to tell his widow that the agency would take care of all her children's college expenses. Another employee was given six months off—with pay—to take care of her terminally ill husband.

In addition to offering financial aid, Burnett also maintains a free employee assistance center (located two blocks away from the office, to ensure confidentiality). The center helps workers deal with depression, grief, divorce, legal problems—"anything," says Evelyn Deiterling, Burnett's benefits manager, "even if an employee just needs someone to talk to."

"People sometimes feel very angry about a death, for example, and their feelings are very hard to sort out. They feel better talking to a stranger who can reassure them that their feelings are normal."

The 3M Company in St. Paul, Minnesota has a formal "survivor's benefit" which provides up to $5,000 to the family of a deceased employee. William Douville, Manager of Survivor Benefits, recalls one employee's widow who wanted to make sure that her husband's three favorite nephews could attend his funeral. "She had no way of knowing if they could afford to pay the airfare, so she wanted to purchase their tickets," Douville says. "That check was delivered on the day we heard of the death."

All 3M employees are eligible for survivor's benefits, regardless of their position in the company. The amount is determined solely by their length of service with the company.

Douville advises managers to leave such matters as arranging benefit payments and family counseling to the professionals, but he feels very strongly about managers being personally supportive. "The biggest statement a manager can make is to show sincere concern by being there and assisting with anything he can," he says.

And, he adds, managers should go to funerals. "We had one instance," he says, "when a man had been on disability from 3M for thirteen years before he passed away. His widow told me that she was deeply touched that in the funeral register was the name of a retired executive secretary who had seen her ex-employee's name in the obituary column. It means so much to the family when co-workers and other people from the company go to the funeral to pay their respects."

Wheeler says, "In any difficult situation, it's up to the manager to set an example, but you also have to take the lead when it's time to get back to business. Help employees deal with their grief when it's appropriate, then go back to work. You and your employees will be better off if you get on with your lives."

Above all, whether dealing with groups or individuals, never forget your personal code of ethics—it is your key to successful relationships and your overall success in life.

—— POSITIVE ACTION STEPS ——

☞ Write down your personal code of ethics.

☞ In a group, make sure every member
is clear on the group's agenda.

☞ Limit groups to the absolute minimum
needed to get the job done.

DAY 12

LEADERS AND THE LED

Men and women can be divided into two classes: the leaders and the led. Unfortunately most of us fall into the category of the led.

Leadership is far more than the ability to boss people around. It is the ability to inspire and excite others with your vision, according to Warren Bennis, a professor of management and organization at the University of Southern California.

After interviewing and observing some ninety leaders in business, public service, the arts, and sports, Bennis concluded, "Unsuccessful leaders are all alike: but every successful leader is successful in his own way."

Bennis told the Chicago *Tribune* that he was floored by the diversity of successful leaders, "I was faced with what I call the Anna Karenina syndrome in reverse," Bennis says, referring to Tolstoy's wisdom about families.

As a consultant to the last four U.S. presidents, Bennis did, however, find one trait common to all. It is what he and others refer to as "vision." "I cannot exaggerate this difference," he told the *Tribune*. "It's as if they are drawing people to them, but it's not necessarily the quality we think of as charisma. It's a kind of laser beam intensity they get when they're talking about their vision. When they're talking about something else, they can be as boring as the next person."

Bennis also found that his subjects were able to communicate their ideas to others. Ronald Reagan's skill has earned him the nickname, "the Great Communicator," but it's an ability Bennis says Jimmy Carter never mastered.

One of Bennis' subjects, Carter's commerce secretary Jaunita Kreps, told him she did not know what Carter was working for as president. "It was like looking at the wrong side of a tapestry," she told Bennis. "Everything was blurry and indistinct."

Good leaders are also persistent. Admiral Hyman Rickover told Bennis that the nuclear submarine never would have been built if he had not kept the idea alive. The effort required, in Rickover's words, "courageous patience" because the idea seemed at first, like so many workable ideas, cockeyed.

A fourth attribute that Bennis observed is a healthy self-respect, out of which grows a profitable respect for others. "Leaders discovered, usually at an early age, what their strengths were and nurtured them. Such leaders are often able to bring out the best in others. They see latent talent and encourage it. They listen to their subordinates, and they realize that a person's inability to do one job does not mean he is incompetent at all jobs," Bennis said.

Not everyone is born to be a team leader, but according to *Fortune* magazine most people can learn the skills it takes to become one.[1] The process, though, may be painful. *Fortune* offers five tips that you may find helpful if you are called on to make the move from a traditional management role to becoming a team leader.

First, don't be afraid to admit that you don't know something. In today's high-tech world, it's virtually impossible for any leader

---

1 "What Team Leaders Need to Know," by Susan Caminiti; *Fortune*, February 20, 1995, 93-100.

to know the details of every team member's job. As the leader, your job is to keep the team functioning smoothly to make sure you deliver a quality product or project on time and on budget.

Second, *Fortune* says, know when to intervene. When you are the team leader, it's your job to lead. Sure, everyone on the team values his or her independence, but when some of the members are stalled or personality conflicts arise, if you don't step in and resolve them, the project may fail. Too little direction can be as fatal as too much.

Third, learn to truly share power. Team leadership really is different from management. A leader's job is to facilitate, to help team members resolve the problems, not solve them himself. You must also be willing to relinquish control and not worry about job security. Trusting others and allowing them to be their best can free you up for more interesting and challenging tasks.

Fourth, worry about what you take on, not what you give up. When you empower your employees, it's normal to fear that you may be empowering yourself out of a job. Don't worry. Good team leaders are always in demand, and you may find yourself teaching others how to make teams work more effectively.

Finally, *Fortune* says, get used to learning on the job. The world is changing so quickly these days that keeping up requires constant learning. In fact, in most jobs, learning is a part of the job. As teams figure out how to operate more efficiently and eliminate unnecessary tasks and paperwork, we will all be required to constantly learn new systems and techniques. You will never know all the answers, but searching for them is half the fun anyway.

POSITIVE ACTION STEPS

☞ Treat those you lead as you would want to be treated.

☞ Motivate with rewards for good service.

☞ Listen to your subordinates. Good ideas can come from anywhere, and others will respect you for hearing them out.

DAY 13

WHAT GOES AROUND COMES AROUND

A very unlikely politician once said that the way to succeed in politics is to live your life so that you wouldn't be embarrassed about anything you've done if it appeared on the front page of the newspaper. It is also a good idea in business.

I have always tried to sit down with every employee at least once a year and give him or her a formal performance evaluation. This shouldn't be the only time you talk, of course, but such a setting encourages both the manager and the managed to talk about major career issues and opportunities for improvement on both sides. No matter how hard you try, though, it doesn't always work.

One company for which I worked had three rankings: below expectation, at expectation, and above expectation. I gave "above expectation" ratings only to the superstars. Excellence was the standard. Quality work got an "at expectation" rating.

Those who were rated "below expectation" should seriously consider other career options. At one of those meetings, I told one of my employees that I had rated him "at expectation." Actually, I felt I was stretching the evaluation a bit. This guy definitely needed some improvement, but I wanted to encourage him rather than demoralize him. Well, the employee was enraged. He was livid. He told me that in all his years with the company, he had never been rated "at expectation." He was an "above expectation" employee, he said.

I explained my policy, the rating standard—all to no avail. Finally the employee said, "I deserve an 'above expectation' rating, and I demand it from you."

As calmly as I could, I responded, "I'm your manager, and how I rate you is my prerogative. I rate you 'at expectation,' although I will tell you that I am rethinking that position."

My employee said, "You will hear from my attorney," and stormed out of the office. Sure enough, a couple of days later I received a phone call from the attorney threatening to sue. I said, "You're going to sue me for giving someone a satisfactory performance evaluation? Get a life, Jack, and get some cases you can win!"

Of course, the suit never materialized, the employee left to take another job, and life went on. A few years later, though, I got a call from a good friend who said, "We just interviewed a former employee of yours, and he's a finalist for one of our top jobs. But he didn't list you as a reference. Any idea why?"

Perhaps that employee could have used the politician's advice about living your life so you wouldn't be ashamed to read about it in the newspaper. The politician's name? It was George Wallace!

If you find yourself in the unenviable position of having to fire such a person, remember, how you let people go says a lot about you—and it can affect the employees left behind. Especially if your staff has had to be trimmed because of some occurrence that is out of their power, like a company merger, divestiture, or takeover. The remaining employees are very likely to feel demoralized, stunned, or scared.

"Today's swiftly changing business environment can erode morale and therefore productivity almost overnight," says the Research Institute of America. "Taking constructive steps to repair the damage and restore the confidence of subordinates can no longer be approvingly recognized by top management as important and then given only lip-service follow-through; rather, tangible steps need to be taken—and taken quickly—after a major change in corporate status." This is what the Research Institute suggests:

☞ **Talk to your staff and be honest**. If the cutbacks have ended, you can raise morale by promising a new future. If the worst is not over, be as straightforward as possible.

☞ **Be a leader**. Let your people know that you are giving them the true picture. Distance yourself from idle gossip and try to form opinions based on insight and facts. To clear the air, answer all the questions you can and listen to grievances from dissenters.

☞ **Begin a new program**. Assign a project that is demanding—something your people can focus on to recapture self-esteem.

☞ **Create a reward system**. Raising salaries may be out of the question, but there might be some other kind of compensation or special recognition that can serve as a substitute to provide emotional support.

☞ **Foster a positive mindset**. Let the survivors see themselves as the cream of the crop, even if they are not. If they sense that they survived because the company needs them for important new projects, they can become winners.

—— POSITIVE ACTION STEPS ——

☞ Never threaten anyone. You never know when it will come back to haunt you.

☞ Avoid spreading rumors and gossip.

☞ Always do your best, and you will never have to worry about defending your actions.

DAY 14

INITIATIVE

We all know that initiative and persistence are essential ingredients of success. It's an easy concept to understand, but one that can be very difficult to put into practice when no one believes in you but you.

Tom Lehman is very hot on the professional golf circuit these days, but for years he fought self-doubt and depression and barely eked out a living. For eight years—five of them in a row—he couldn't qualify for the PGA Tour, and it was just six years ago that he was ready to quit golf altogether. He was so discouraged that he applied for a job as golf coach at his alma mater, the University of Minnesota, at a salary of twenty-nine thousand dollars a year. But he still struggled on the professional golf circuit.

He told golf writer Jeff Rude in an article in Northwest Airline's *World Traveler* magazine that he couldn't remember ever having more than four or five thousand dollars in the bank. Then something happened. It didn't come in a blinding flash of light with a message written in the clouds. It was much more mundane.

Late in 1990, with very little money in the bank, as he struggled to make the cut in the PGA Tour Qualifying Tournament finals, his caddie said something that changed his life. He said, "Why don't you just play like a champion."

Lehman made the cut. By 1992, his earnings on the PGA Tour were well into six figures, and in 1994 he passed the one million dollar mark. He came close to winning the Masters Tournament in 1994, and Rude reports that Lehman now believes he has the potential to be the best.

"It's gotten to the point now," Lehman said in *World Traveler*, "that if I play well, I've got a chance to win any tournament."

Success in any field usually comes at a very high cost. If you study the lives of great achievers, you will often discover that they—like Tom Lehman—tried and failed many times before making it big. They worked long after the others had given up and gone home, preparing themselves so they would be ready when their time came. That's the power of persistence.

The engine that drives success is personal discipline. It is the willpower, the determination, the strength of character that compels you to stay with the job until it is finished. Most important, it is the personality trait that sustains you when you take charge of your life. If you are a disciplined person, you know you can react positively to the most negative situation—you can handle whatever comes your way.

There is no easy way to develop personal discipline. It is the result of forcing yourself to do the right thing, to take the initiative to accomplish something when you'd much rather be doing something else.

Personal discipline is developed one act and one day at a time until it becomes a habit to listen to your inner voice when it tells you to get going and take positive action instead of procrastinating and putting off until tomorrow what you should be doing today. Developing personal discipline is made more difficult because discipline does not usually provide instant gratification. In fact, the first feedback you receive may be negative as others try to persuade you to forget about work and do something that is more fun. Nevertheless, if you stick with it, the rewards of personal discipline do eventually come.

Those who can discipline themselves to perform difficult tasks, to do what needs to be done regardless of what others may say, are the people who earn the respect and big promotions. They become the leaders.

Making the decision to change your life is the easy part. Getting the job done is a lengthy, lonely, tedious process that requires a commitment that will sustain you no matter how tough things get or how much you are tempted. The habits you're trying to change have been developed gradually over a long period of time, and they will be eliminated the same way. In fact, most of us don't recognize our habits as such until they are so firmly ingrained that they are extremely difficult to break.

Self-help groups recognize how difficult it is to make a major change in your lifestyle, and they use a variety of techniques—peer pressure, reinforcement, group discussion—to aid the process. Nevertheless, in the end it is always an individual matter.

We must break habits the same way we formed them: one drink, one cigarette, or one Twinkie at a time. To think that we must immediately stop drinking, smoking, overeating, or indulging in any unhealthy or destructive habit is overwhelming at first. Instead, we vow that we won't drink the next cocktail, smoke the next cigarette, or eat the next candy bar. We know we can avoid one destructive behavior; beyond that we're not sure.

Like any goal in life, changing your behavior is something you have to work at slowly, one small step at a time. But if you're dedicated to your goal, you can achieve it.

POSITIVE ACTION STEPS

☞ Always do more than you're paid to do.

☞ Break old habits by replacing them
with new, good habits.

☞ Build good habits one day at a time.

CHAPTER THREE

KNOWLEDGE IS POWER

Today, gathering information is not a problem. We are bombarded with it. Week Three focuses on how to assimilate and use knowledge to its best advantage.

DAY 15

CREATING YOUR OWN FUTURE

If you have no plan for achieving your goals, they're not goals, they're fantasies. In order to achieve a goal you first need a precise plan broken down into specific things that you must accomplish in the short, medium, and long term.

Let's say, for example, that your goal is to become the top salesperson in your company. Your short-term objective would be to sell enough to put you at the top of the list this week. A medium-term objective would be to become the top salesperson each month. In the long term, the objective would involve being the best this year and repeat the process and improve on it every year thereafter. All activities would be directed toward the actions necessary to reach each milestone.

For instance, good salespeople keep records of the number of qualified prospects they contact to request an appointment to make a sales presentation. They also track the actual number of appointments, presentations, and sales that result. Over time they develop averages that can be used to project future sales.

They learn that in order to achieve a desired sales level, they must make the required number of calls. If they simply make the calls, sales will follow. The averages will hold—and even improve—as the salesperson's skills improve. Such knowledge greatly reduces stress and minimizes the uncertainty of selling.

If salespeople simply pay attention to the basics and do the right things, they will earn the incomes they deserve.

Of course, this technique works with anything that is measurable. If you wish to lose weight, for example, establish an overall goal of losing a certain number of pounds, and determine how much you must lose each week to meet your goal.

Without a clear vision of what you wish to achieve, you may be easily distracted and soon forget what you set out to accomplish. Setting a goal helps you focus all your thoughts and energy on what you wish to achieve. It ensures that you do not fall into an activity trap—assuming that just because you're busy that you must be accomplishing something.

A goal also keeps you on course when the playing field changes or unexpected events occur along the way. Such things may temporarily delay or deflect you from your objective, but if you have your goal firmly in mind, nothing can deter you for long. Obstacles become merely temporary inconveniences to be overcome.

There are four basic elements to a goal: 1) a clear, concise written statement of what you wish to achieve; 2) a plan for achieving your goal; 3) a timetable for achieving your goal; and 4) a commitment to achieve the goal regardless of the obstacles to be overcome.

Perhaps the most important element of a goal is writing it down. Thoughts are often vague and imprecise, while a written sentence requires you to choose correct words and be specific.

We learn in school at a very early age that when the teacher says something is important, we should write it down because we very likely will be tested on the topic. Throughout our lives and careers, that message is reinforced—almost everything important should eventually be committed to writing. Writing down a goal also helps internalize it.

Learning experts say that using more than one sense—hearing, seeing, touching, smelling, and tasting—facilitates learning and helps the memory process. Our thinking is clarified and our recollection of precisely what we wish to achieve is greatly enhanced by writing it down, studying it, and memorizing it.

Your written goal need not be long. In fact, the shorter it is, the better. Limit your goal to a sentence or two at most and make sure it is easily understood. A good rule is: If it won't fit on a three-by-five index card, it's too long. If you require that much verbiage, you are not sufficiently focused.

Take time to think your goals through and condense them into understandable, action-oriented sentences. Repeat your goal to yourself aloud at least a dozen times a day. And always carry your three-by-five card along with you. Every time you see it, it will remind you of your goal and get your mind working again on how to achieve it.

—— **POSITIVE ACTION STEPS** ——

☞ Write down your goals.

☞ Write out a plan for achieving your goal. Break it down into short-, medium-, and long-range objectives.

☞ Repeat your goal aloud at least a
dozen times each day.

DAY 16

THE VALUE OF
EXPERIENCE

These days in business, you don't have to look very far to find a crisis. A lawsuit, a product recall, an injury at the plant, a strike, criminal or bizarre behavior by an employee—just about anything can put you in the public eye briefly in this talk show world we live in. The best advice I've ever gotten on how to deal with such problems comes from my friend Dick Hyde, an executive with a large public relations firm.

Hyde had his first experience with crisis communications on the Three Mile Island fiasco, and he's dealt with some other pretty high profile problems since. His advice? Tell the truth, tell it all, and tell it quickly. When you do, it becomes a non-story. It's far more interesting to read about a cover-up than about some-body who made a mistake, took responsibility for it, and fixed the problem. You can also take heart in the fact that although your newfound notoriety may be exceedingly painful for you and the employees of your company, most of the world will little note nor long remember your problems.

A few years ago, the company I worked for was involved in a very visible lawsuit that the major metropolitan newspaper in the city had a vested interest in. Not only did they cover us as news, they wrote editorials about how badly we'd handled the situation. When it was finally over, I remarked to a good friend that I was greatly relieved to have that situation behind me. And he said, "What was that about again; I must have missed it."

As the old journalist said, "Don't get too caught up in the publicity. Today's news is tomorrow's fish wrapper."

Through experience you will find that generally there is no mistake too great for you to rise above. There is no setback you can't overcome.

Even great people make mistakes. Thomas Edison was one of the world's most spectacular failures. He tried more than 10,000 experiments in his attempt to develop the incandescent light. Imagine what would have happened if he had quit after just a few tries.

Cowboys in the Old West had a colorful expression for sticking with the job until it was done: "There never was a horse that couldn't be rode, and there never was a cowboy that couldn't be throwed." They knew that sometimes you win and sometimes you lose and that some things require more effort than others, but if you persist, you will eventually prevail.

Cowboys also knew that the best time to get back on the horse was immediately after you had been thrown—while the lesson is still clear in your mind.

Here are a few questions you can ask yourself to help guide you in learning from your mistakes. Ask yourself:

1. Why did I fail to do what I expected? Was it because I was poorly prepared, lacked a certain skill, or had unrealistic expectations?

2. What did I learn from the experience that I can constructively apply in the future?

3. Did external factors over which I had little or no control affect the outcome? If so, what were those factors, and how can I minimize them in the future?

4. What could I have done differently to minimize the risk of failure?

5. What knowledge or skill do I need to ensure that I do not make the same mistake again?

6. How will I obtain that knowledge or skill?

7. Who can I call upon to help me obtain the knowledge or skill I need to succeed?

8. Who has an interest in my success and would be willing to help me?

9. What action should I take to ensure success next time?

10. Why should I continue to try until I succeed? What are the rewards for success compared to the penalties for failure?

Once you have examined your mistake in this way, you are stronger, better prepared, and more likely to succeed next time. The worst thing you can do is give up without a fight.

Calvin Coolidge once made this observation: "Nothing in the world can take the place of persistence. Talent will not; for nothing is more common than unsuccessful people with talent. Genius will not. For unheralded Genius is almost a proverb. Education will not: for the world is full of educated derelicts. Persistence and determination alone are supreme."

— POSITIVE ACTION STEPS —

☞ Seek out the most experienced person in your field, and learn from him or her.

☞ Give others the benefit of your experience.

☞ Don't dwell on your mistakes—almost nothing will teach you as much as a good mistake will.

DAY 17

ACCURATE THINKING

The human brain has often been compared to a computer, and in many ways it is similar. Both can store and process information, but there is one significant difference in the methods they use.

As long as information is put into a computer's memory in a consistent fashion, data can be organized, compared, and extracted intact. In the human computer of our memories, on the other hand, the data may be clouded by emotions, biases, prejudices, or the simple passage of time. Yet it is absolutely essential that if we are to make the correct decisions in the wildly varying circumstances that we often face in our lives, we must be able to think clearly and accurately.

The best method might be to approach all the so-called facts with a healthy skepticism. Recognize from the start that things are not always what they seem. Ask yourself some questions: Do the facts support this expert's opinion? Is it corroborated by others in the field? Is his or her opinion consistent with my own experience, knowledge, and training? Does it make good common sense?

Accurate thinking is assisted by what W. Clement Stone calls the R2A2 formula. Simply stated, the R2A2 formula is to recognize and relate, assimilate and apply the information learned in any field to solve the problem at hand.

Accurate thinkers learn to trust their own judgment and to be cautious no matter who tries to influence them. They learn to listen to the words and to study the body language, to examine their instinctive reactions that tell them to be careful about getting involved with one person or another. They learn to trust their intuition.

There's an old story about a law school professor who was so rigid in demanding that his students confine themselves to known facts and not to engage in speculation of any kind that the students decided to play a trick on the professor. They somehow managed to acquire a white horse which they then very carefully painted black on one side and left the other side white. They then took the two-tone horse to a field near the university, and assigned one member of the group to stand with the horse and position it so that only the black side faced the road. Next they drove the professor to the field and asked: "What do you see?"

The professor replied: "I see Mr. Thomas holding the halter of a horse, the side of which is facing me is apparently black."

It is a good idea to make sure that things are indeed what they seem when you make important decisions. That means that in order to accurately assess your situation, besides mere facts, you must be able to put things like adversity, defeat, and constancy of purpose into proper perspective.

Adversity is not something to be feared; there is opportunity in every adversity. In fact, consultants who study such things report that customers who have a problem that is solved to their satisfaction become more loyal customers than those who have never had a problem at all. Also, those customers usually tell everyone they know about their experience. They also tell everyone they know when they have had an unhappy experience that was not resolved to their satisfaction. When you lose a customer because he or she is unhappy with your performance, you can be sure that a lot of other people will know about it.

The seed of opportunity in such adversities lies in the fact that every unhappy customer is really an opportunity to create a customer for life. Treating the customer right always pay big dividends.

Dealing with defeat can be a little tougher. But while the circumstances of life are such that everyone must undergo a certain amount of temporary defeat, you can find hope in the knowledge that every such defeat also carries with it the seed of equivalent or greater benefit. Things to remember are:

- ☞ Defeat may be a stepping stone or a stumbling block, according to the mental attitude in which one relates himself to it.

- ☞ Defeat may reveal to you powers that you never knew you possessed.

- ☞ Defeat is never the same as failure unless and until it has been accepted as such.

Adversity and defeat are both things that can be conquered through constancy of purpose. Napoleon Hill wrote, "Constancy of purpose is the first principle of success."

He pointed out that it is critical to our success that we have a well thought-out plan for our lives and that we stick with it regardless of what others may say and the obstacles we may encounter. There will always be faultfinders and those who attempt to persuade us that our goals aren't worth the effort we put into achieving them. But those people will never go far, and they will be the first to ask for your help after you have passed them by.

Virtually every successful person has considered giving up at some point in his or her struggle to reach the top. And many breakthroughs occurred soon after those same people rededicated themselves to their purpose. There is no known obstacle that cannot be overcome by a person who has constancy of purpose, a positive mental attitude, and the discipline and willpower to succeed. You can do it if you only believe you can.

——— POSITIVE ACTION STEPS ———

☞ Look for the opportunity in every adversity. It is there.

☞ View defeat as merely a learning process.

☞ Never be rushed into a decision. If you can't have time to think about it, forget it.

DAY 18

CRIPPLING KINDNESS

How many times have you taken advice from well-meaning people only to discover later that you have been crippled by what you accepted as their generosity?

In the *New York Times* book review section,[2] South African poet and painter Breyten Breytenbach recalled a story about a black man who was born before the abolition of slavery.

Freedom, as the old man was known, was once the property of a one-legged slave holder. Whenever the owner bought new shoes, he gave the left one to his slave, having no use for it himself.

Freedom saved the shoe until he had two new left shoes so he would have a "pair." Wearing left shoes on both his left and right feet was not only a little uncomfortable, but it eventually impaired Freedom's right foot, causing him to hobble painfully throughout his later life. He was permanently crippled by the "generosity" of his master.

In today's world it is more important than ever to think for ourselves, to adopt the uncommon habit of common sense. People love to give you advice on how to do things. Many are quick to criticize a new idea, to tell you why what you want to do won't work, or encourage you to give up because that's what they would do in your situation.

---

2   *New York Times*, March 28, 1993; Book Review.

Without a grounding philosophy to guide you, you may be easily misled by others. They may be acting with the best of intentions because they actually believe they know better than you do how you should live your life. But deep down, you know what is right for you. In fact, you are the only one who can know what's right for you.

Listen carefully to the advice you get from others, but never be afraid to discard that which runs contrary to your goals in life. When you blindly follow the advice of others, whatever their motivation, you run the risk of never reaching your goals, your true potential, and in the long run you may permanently cripple yourself.

Of course, there are times when you must accept the fact that you can't do everything for yourself. There are certain circumstances when you will be far more effective if you seek professional help from those who can best assist you.

When you do decide that you need professional help, be careful to choose the right firm or person for the job.

Most professional societies maintain lists of their members, but they will tell you little more than whether or not the person in question is a member in good standing. The American Medical Association, for example, won't tell you that your doctor has a long list of malpractice complaints lodged against him or her, just as the American Society of Certified Public Accountants will not offer an opinion about the competence of its members. Being a member in good standing simply means that the individual has completed the necessary educational requirements and passed the appropriate examinations to be certified or licensed to practice in your state.

So how do you check them out? Start with your Better Business Bureau. They can tell you whether or not clients have filed complaints about an individual or group, what types of complaints, and how many.

Next, ask for referrals. Ask your friends and neighbors who prepares their taxes or to which doctor they take their kids. You may not even have to ask. Most of us like to recommend those who do outstanding work, and we don't hesitate to complain to others if we are dissatisfied. In fact, market researchers who study such things tell us if a consumer is dissatisfied with a product or service, he or she will tell somewhere between ten and twenty friends, while they will tell only approximately one-third that number if they are happy with a product or service.

Finally, and most unscientifically, trust your instincts. If you don't have confidence in a person, don't retain him or her. You must often tell this person intimate details about your finances, your body, your failures—very private things—and if you are not comfortable with the individual, you may withhold critical information. You may hurt yourself by making it difficult for the professionals to do their best for you.

Ask lots of questions. If professionals can't answer a question to your satisfaction in a language you can understand, or if they patronize you, forget them. Find someone who will answer your questions—after all, that's why you hired them.

—— POSITIVE ACTION STEPS ——

☞ When someone tells you what you should or shouldn't
do, ask yourself objectively: Will this action help
me toward my goal or take me away from it?

☞ Don't let others tell you can't reach your goal. They
said the same thing to Edison and the Wright Brothers.

☞ Being a professional doesn't make an
individual perfect. Ask about everything
until you are satisfied with the answers.

DAY 19

SATISFIED CUSTOMERS

Being really successful may require more than just keeping up with what's new in your industry or profession. It may also require a healthy dose of common sense.

I once worked for a trade association that, as part of its membership services, offered to arbitrate disputes between members of the association and customers. If they couldn't resolve a disagreement themselves, we would try to help. It never ceased to amaze me that two views of a single experience could be so vastly different. In fact, the differences were sometimes so astounding that I felt compelled to confirm that we were talking about the same event.

Those experiences gave me a keen appreciation for the importance of expectation management—of making sure that your customers know exactly how much they are spending and what they expect to receive in return. If these two items aren't clearly understood by both parties, trouble isn't far behind.

If top executives of every organization spent a few hours each week working in the customer service department, many complaints about service and product quality would quickly be fixed.

Smart managers know there is value in the unhappy customer.

A couple of weeks ago I went to a restaurant I sometimes frequent for lunch. I chose this place because I didn't have much cash with me, and I knew they accepted credit cards. When I got there, I was told by the waiter that they no longer accepted credit cards. As I was about to leave, the manager who had overheard the conversation stopped me. She said that just because I didn't know about their new policy was no reason I had to miss lunch. So they bought my lunch.

It was only the cost of the lunch, but now they have a customer for life. And I must have told that story to more than twenty people.

We can all learn from that manager. If, despite our best efforts, a customer has a problem and we can fix it, we have an opportunity to make him a bigger and better customer than if he never had a problem.

Sometimes, though, you have to listen carefully to know there is a problem or concern.

I once worked for a guy who said, "When you can figure out what keeps your clients awake at night, you can make a lot of money selling solutions that give them peace of mind." To identify those problems that your clients or customers worry about most, you have to listen to them.

Listening is hard work, as Kerry L. Johnson points out in *Sales Magic: Revolutionary New Techniques That Will Double Your Sales Volume in 21 Days*, published by William Morrow and Company, Inc. Listening requires active concentration and focus. Johnson identifies eight steps of active listening. They are:

I. **Value the speaker**. When you are talking to someone, that individual is the most important person in the world.

2. **Pay attention to what is not said**. Sometimes what is left out of the discussion is more important than what is included.

3. **Try to hear the truth**. Set aside any preconceived notions that you may have and listen to the what is being said, not who is saying it.

4. **Limit the time you speak**. We live in a sound bite world. Television advertisers know that we have an attention span of about 30 seconds. Use this knowledge to your advantage.

5. **Avoid the tendency to think about what you will say after your customers stop talking**. A conversation isn't merely two or more people taking turns talking. Actively listen to what is being said.

6. **Listen to your customer's point of view**. Recognize that we are all unique with an individual perception of the world. Listen for the thoughts behind the words to understand your customer's point of view.

7. **Repeat your clients' comments to make sure they know you heard what they said**. Repeating the message helps avoid misunderstandings, clarify issues, and helps embed the information in your mind.

8. **Don't take extensive notes while listening**. Too much note taking interrupts eye contact and breaks rapport with the speaker. Take only cryptic notes that remind you of agreed-upon action steps.

Regardless of our station in life, we can all benefit from advice that helps us become better listeners. Active listening can enhance all kinds of relationships—business, professional, and personal. After all, we are all selling something: an idea, a dream, a budget, a project, or ourselves.

—— POSITIVE ACTION STEPS ——

☞ When someone is not satisfied with your work or your product, set about fixing it as if your livelihood depended on it—because it does.

☞ Say what you mean, and mean what you say.

☞ Learn to listen at least as much as you talk.

DAY 20

CONTROLLED ATTENTION

An ordinary light bulb and the laser both emit light. But what gives the laser the power to cut through metal? In part, it's due to the tight focus of the laser.

The same principle of focus or controlled attention can help you achieve laser-like performance. Napoleon Hill defined the principle of controlled attention as the ability, through habit and practice, to keep your mind on one subject until you have thoroughly familiarized yourself with it and mastered it. It means the ability to focus your attention on a given problem until you have it solved.

Controlled attention is also the ability to manage your thoughts and direct them to a definite end. It is the ability to organize your knowledge into a plan of action that is sound and workable.

You will achieve your goals when you focus your thoughts on a definite, written, realistic plan of action and imagine yourself in the position of having accomplished what you set out to do.

Hill reminds us that nothing was ever created by any human being that was not first created in the imagination then, through a burning desire and controlled attention, transformed into reality. When you really concentrate on a goal and see yourself as you wish to become in one, two, three, five, or ten years—earning the income you desire, owning the new home you want, a person of means and influence—you begin to become that person. If you paint this picture clearly in your imagination, it will soon become the object of a deep desire. Use that desire to control your attention and drive you into action and you can accomplish things you thought were impossible.

Action is a key word. Many times we have the desire to succeed, but fail to act because of the fear of making a wrong decision.

Everyone has difficulty making decisions occasionally. We don't want to make a hasty judgment on something really important, but we don't want indecisiveness to immobilize us either.

Here a few practical tips that may be helpful in being decisive without resorting to snap judgments:

First, take your time with important decisions. Seldom do they have to be made instantly. Sleep on it. You are more objective twenty-four hours later.

Second, recognize that life is not made up of true/false or multiple-choice questions. Usually there are several answers, any one of which may be considered "right" or "wrong."

Third, remember that every decision has consequences. Determining what they are will help you make an informed decision.

Fourth, make sure you put the decision in proper context. All decisions are not equal. If the consequences are insignificant, the situation merits very little concern.

Fifth, be aware that no one else can make decisions for you. Never let another person decide important matters for you, and don't blame them for a failed attempt when things go wrong. Your decisions are yours alone. Accept responsibility for them.

Last, keep in mind that seldom are decisions irrevocable. If you make the wrong one, usually you can go back and fix it.

After you've made your decision, give it time to work. Don't give up or change your mind just because things do not immediately work out the way you expected. Most things take time, particularly when other people are involved. Because you are excited about a new idea or opportunity does not mean others will automatically follow suit. They may be envious or they may simply not care one way or the other. If it was a good decision yesterday, the chances are good that it will still be solid today and tomorrow.

Remember that you've had time to think things through; you've done your homework. Give others the same opportunity. Usually, they will come around. But even if you have to go it alone, if you have made a careful, thoughtful, informed decision, you will have the courage of your convictions. Knowing you are right will keep you strong when the going gets tough—and it most always does. Go the extra mile to make sure that you give your idea or opportunity a fair chance. Those who achieve the most in life are people who give more than what is expected of them.

—— **POSITIVE ACTION STEPS** ——

☞ Spend a few minutes three times a day
envisioning yourself achieving your ultimate
goal (i.e. wealth, new car, etc.).

☞ Realize that you can do just about
anything—if you believe you can.

☞ When you face a difficult decision, sleep on it.

DAY 21

ANTICIPATING CHANGE

A chieving success may at first appear to be mostly happenstance or luck. But when you know the key, you will discover that what may have seemed like random chance is really part of a grand design.

W. Clement Stone uses the Rosetta Stone as an example. Until it was discovered in 1799, Egyptian hieroglyphics appeared to be little more than random etchings of a primitive people. With the key—the Rosetta Stone—scholars were able to decipher the real meaning of the symbols. So it is with success.

Without the key, success seems to be just random happenings. But with the key, you can take steps to make success happen.

Stone says, here is the key: First, remember that all achievement begins with a clear mental image of one's goal—a definite picture of what you desire from life. Second, this picture is translated into action through personal initiative.

If the chosen goal is beyond attainment for one person, the services of others are utilized through what has been called the "master mind," a completely harmonious partnership in which the education, experience, influence, and occasionally the working capital of each member complements and supplements the other members.

Next, to achieve success you must be willing to go the extra mile—to do more than you are paid to do. To make this happen, you need a positive mental attitude.

If you can conceive and believe it, you can achieve it. Develop the complete belief that you can do anything you set out to do.

This requires applied faith—the power to draw on spiritual resources endowed to us by our Creator. Your faith, then, can help you develop accurate thinking—the ability to think clearly, separating fact from fiction.

Accurate thinking requires controlled attention or the ability to concentrate on your definite goal with persistence. This in turn demands self-discipline.

Through self-discipline you develop the power to turn on more willpower, rather than quitting, when you run into obstacles. With it you will learn how to budget time and money.

You'll also need good physical and mental health habits because a healthy mind will give you enthusiasm—perhaps the most essential trait for the successful person. With enthusiasm you can develop a pleasing personality through which others will lend you their friendly cooperation in attaining your goal and your creative vision.

With creative vision, you will be able to learn from defeat, where every adversity carries with it "the seed of an equivalent benefit."

Like the Rosetta Stone links the hieroglyphics and gives them meaning, the principles of success are similarly linked. One leads to the other, and together they lead to success. This is true no matter how times and circumstances change. Armed with this knowledge, you have no reason to fear change.

Even though we all know that change is an essential element of human progress, it is the one thing which many people fight hardest.

Napoleon Hill said that the law of change is inexorable. Countless civilizations have died for violating it. For the law reads that just as the physical world must undergo incessant change, man's social and cultural world must progress or die.

Though the law is harsh and unyielding, it is actually a blessing in disguise. Without change, man would still be an animal. With change and an understanding of success principles, he can map his own earthly destiny and create the ways and means of attaining it.

Despite repeated attempts at self-destruction, mankind somehow seems to learn from mistakes and retain the best elements of civilizations that have gone on before. The ancient Greeks bequeathed a great deal to us in art, philosophy, and architecture; and much of our modern legal system is based on Roman law. We have even seen some periods of world peace during the course of history. And all of this amounts to change for the better.

You can also use the law of change to achieve your own individual aims of material success. Fatalism is insufficient. You must take positive steps to make events work out the way you want them. And you must do it in full faith that what you wish will come to pass if your goal is a proper one.

Hill said, "Recognition of the law of change can also ease the blows that life deals out to you. Even the loss of a loved one will be softened by acknowledgment that grief itself is something that must and will pass away. Don't resist the law of change, make it work for you."

Henry Ford should have known more than any man of his time that the law of change demands persistent progress. But he once lost sight of that fact—and almost lost his business.

A stubborn man, Ford refused to believe that the Model "T" could ever be supplanted despite repeated warnings from his associates. Competitors proved Ford wrong, and his sales dropped dangerously before he realized his error and recouped with new, modern methods.

Like Ford himself, the company that he founded has made its share of miscalculations over the years, but it has enjoyed some notable success as well. Today's Ford executives follow in a long tradition of innovation in the automobile industry, and the Ford name is known around the world as a maker of fine, affordable automobiles. Change is inevitable. And you must be prepared to seize the opportunities offered you through change—or doom yourself to failure.

—— POSITIVE ACTION STEPS ——

☞ Develop a clear mental image of your goal, one that is so vivid it can be recalled to help you through temporary setbacks.

☞ Exercise regularly—a healthy body actually will help you maintain a healthy mind.

☞ Stop fighting change. Instead, explore ways to take advantage of it.

CHAPTER FOUR

A FEW WHO DARED

There are countless excuses for not succeeding, but success is achieved by those who refuse to accept defeat. Their stories prove that it is possible to overcome the odds, and they inspire us to persevere. Following are the stories of a few successful people whose lives serve as a beacon of hope to all those who are still struggling to find their way.

DAY 22

AGAINST ALL ODDS—
MIKE UTLEY

On November 17, 1991, in a game between the Detroit Lions and the Los Angeles Rams, thousands of fans at the stadium and millions more who watched on television breathed a sigh of relief when Lions offensive tackle Mike Utley flashed a "thumbs up" as he was carried off the field.

Despite his reassuring gesture, subsequent medical examinations would confirm Utley's worst fears. While running a pass blocking play, the 6-foot 6-inch, 310-pound offensive tackle had broken his neck and damaged his spinal cord.

"I've been hurt many times before," he recalled. "I've broken bones, I've had 'stingers' when I pinched something in my neck and I've been knocked out. But this time I knew I was in trouble. Something was wrong with my neck, and my legs were burning so bad they felt like they were on fire."

The prognosis was not good. Utley's legs were completely paralyzed and he couldn't lift a napkin with his hands. Doctors told him that he could expect to spend the rest of his life in a wheelchair. They told Utley that he was in a window of healing. If feeling in his arms and legs didn't return during the first six months, it probably wouldn't return at all.

Six months passed, and nothing happened. Then one day, Utley discovered he could move his left big toe. After that, Utley says, things really started to happen. Today, his hands and lower back muscles are functional, he can lift his feet, and he works out with weights almost every day.

In the months and weeks that followed Utley's accident, he received more than 10,000 letters of support from around the world. One in particular touched him. It was from a boy who wrote: "Dear Mr. Utley: I'm sorry you got hurt. If I could switch my legs for yours, I would, so I could watch you play just one more game."

Utley has been a competitor as long as he can remember. "My dad tells a story about when we four kids would wrestle with him. I was the first one there and the last one to leave. I enjoy the physical contact and the competition. I want to be the best. The day I stop competing will be the day they lay me six feet under."

Utley understands well the value of goal setting, something he says he has done every day of his life. "If your goal is to get to the SuperBowl, then you have to break your goals down. In the off season, you start by getting yourself into shape. During the preseason, you spend your time getting the plays down. Then you take the games one at a time, and the next thing you know, you're at the SuperBowl."

"People ask me if I have a grudge against football because of what's happened to me. I tell them, 'Heck, no.' Football put me in this wheelchair, that's true, but football is going to teach me to get out of this chair. Football teaches you to get along with other people, and it teaches you how to be aggressive when you have work to do," Utley said.

"My goal is to one day walk again," he said. "If I don't do it today, I'll do it tomorrow." Utley's first goal when he was in the hospital was to sit up; the next was to stand for a minute. Gradually, he improved until his goal was to be able to stand for an hour. He worked at it for three months, often passing out every time he stood up. It took a bet with his older brother, Tom, to make it past an hour.

"I was up to 47 minutes," Utley recalled, "and that was the longest I'd made it. That lasted for about a month, and all of a sudden I got so mad that I just stood there. People said, 'You look green; you'd better lie down,' but I made it. Tom paid off on the dinner.

"I make bets all the time. I bet myself. I think if you set out to do something, then do it! Do everything a little bit better every day. If you stop and look around, someone is going to pass you up. I won't be passed up. Not now, not ever. That's the way I look at things. If you're going to make a mistake, make it while you're going a million miles an hour. No one can fault you for trying."

These days, Mike Utley lives in Denver but spends much of his time touring the country talking to groups and raising money for the foundation that bears his name. "When I go out and speak, I always tell people to be the best they can be with what they have," he says. "Don't complain about your situation; you only make it worse by complaining."

He recalls how when the Lions were doing six weeks of double practices, team members would grouse and complain as they walked up the hill to the practice field for the second time in a day, "But when we got to the top of the hill, we knew that we still had to practice.

"That's what you call constructive (complaining)—when you know you still have a job to do, and you'll get it done. The other kind is negative. That's just a waste of time and air."

POSITIVE ACTION STEPS

☞ Never give in. No matter how big the
setback, you can overcome it.

☞ Don't bother complaining; it's just a waste of hot air.

☞ Give everything your best shot. No
one can fault you for trying.

DAY 23

FAMOUS AND FORTUNE— WALLY AMOS

I don't see temporary setbacks as obstacles; I think they are really stepping stones." So says the man many call the father of the gourmet cookie industry, a guy who has made a career of turning lemons into lemonade, the ever optimistic Wally Amos.

Amos likes the lemons into lemonade metaphor so much that in his official portrait he holds a glass of lemonade in one hand and a pitcher in the other. His name is a household word, yet because of a lawsuit with the owners of the cookie company he founded, he can't even use his own name in connection with any cookie. But Amos doesn't see this problem as an obstacle.

In a recent interview he said, "As far as I'm concerned, the judge in the case gave me *good* news. Sure, he said that there are a few names I can't use, but look at all the names I *can* use!"

So Wally started a new company he calls "Uncle Noname," which he says is sort of Hawaiian for no name.

A man on what he describes as a permanent spiritual quest, Amos says, "All of life is a divine order. Each of us is a piece of the puzzle, and you don't know where the other pieces are—so you have to be open-minded. You have to be receptive to answers coming from every direction. There's a great quote that I saw at a church at home that says, 'The mind is like a parachute. It functions best when opened.'

"The idea to create Famous Amos was not my idea," he said. "It was an idea that was inspired by God. It just came through me. God gave me the idea. I'm not dealing with a one-idea God. If he gave me the idea for Famous Amos, he'll give me another idea."

The idea for the name of his new company came when he least expected it from a totally unexpected source. He was planning to call it, "Nonamos" to play on the Amos connection until a chance meeting at the beach occurred. As Amos and his wife, Christine, walked along Laguna Beach, a man who had heard him on the radio approached the couple and struck up a conversation.

"His name was Dick Dunchock," Amos recalled, "and he said I should call my new company, 'Noname.' It turned out that he had some printing done at one of those instant printing places and they had forgotten his name. When he went in to pick up his printing, they had written on the order, 'Dick Noname.' the more we talked, the more it seemed like a good idea. The company was named on the beach by a total stranger. This is not a coincidence," Amos said.

The cookie caper was not Amos' first setback. He began his career as a talent scout at the William Morris Agency where he signed an unknown duo named Simon and Garfunkle. He quit William Morris when he sensed that his opportunity for advancement had run its course.

He then went into business for himself, but problems began mounting when clients wouldn't pay their bills.

Amos had had enough. Show business was just too fragile and unstable. It was at the suggestion of a friend that he decided to sell the trademark chocolate chip cookies that for years had served as his calling card with producers and Hollywood executives. Amos persuaded show business friends Helen Reddy, Marvin Gaye, and others to invest in the operation and he was in business.

After a few years, the company began to experience management problems, and Famous Amos went through a series of owners, each diluting Amos' equity. By the time the third set of owners took over, Arnos was a contract employee responsible mostly for promoting the product. He was unable to come to terms with the fourth owners and left the company shortly after they took over.

Today, Amos is as positive as ever, on the road doing what he does best: promoting cookie sales. The Costco Wholesale chain has picked up Uncle Noname cookies and booked Amos for a series of personal appearances.

Amos has a five-point formula for success that anyone can use.

First, There is always an answer. Don't waste your time worrying. Worry is not preparation. Analyze the situation and focus on solutions, you will find that there is always an answer.

Second, Amos says, do something. Action begets action and activity begets activity.

Third, don't become a victim. Don't allow yourself to become angry or frustrated.

Fourth, maintain a positive mental attitude. He says, "If I can lose my name, get fifteen months behind on my mortgage, owe everybody, and still start a new company and keep my positive mental attitude, anybody can."

Fifth, Amos says: Have the courage of your convictions. Trust in yourself and in God. Have the trust and the faith to let go and not agonize over temporary setbacks. Doing it all yourself is a tall order, but with God, all things are possible.

"We aren't making money yet, Amos said, "but the new company will be successful. I am going to be out here promoting until the time comes that when people ask for a chocolate chip cookie, they will say, 'Give me a Noname'!"

I, for one, don't doubt it for a minute.

—— POSITIVE ACTION STEPS ——

☞ The next time you suffer a setback, focus on what to do next instead of wasting time thinking about what just happened.

☞ Maintain a positive mental attitude. You can accomplish anything if you believe you can.

☞ Give yourself time to achieve your goals. Nothing great was ever accomplished overnight.

DAY 24

UPS AND DOWNS— ELISHA OTIS' PERSISTENCE

A great idea alone isn't nearly enough to make you success-ful. Barrooms and locker rooms everywhere are filled with would-be achievers who dream of greatness, but give up too easily.

Elisha Graves Otis had a great idea for a braking system for an elevator, but he quickly learned that having a breakthrough idea was worthless if he couldn't "break through" the complacency of those who had a vested interest in the status quo.

At the time, freight hoists were already in fairly widespread use, but most people wouldn't ride in them because they were afraid the rope would break. As a result, it was generally agreed that the maximum height for a building would always be limited to the four or five stories most people could conveniently climb.

In 1852, Otis built a freight hoist for the Yonkers (New York) Bedstead Manufacturing Company where he was a master mechanic, but he made one small deviation from standard pro-cedure. He added a simple braking device. Otis immediately recognized the benefits the elevator offered; the problem was, nobody else seemed to notice or care.

A year or so after he invented the clever little braking device and started his own company to manufacture elevators, he was still struggling to get attention for his idea. Finally, in one of the most brilliant public relations moves in American business history, Otis built a tower at the first-ever World's Fair, which opened in New York in 1853. As thousands of spectators held their breath, he climbed to the top of the tower, stood on the elevator platform and shouted the command to the workman below: "Cut the rope."

The worker swung his ax, and catapulted Elisha Graves Otis into the history books. His brake held and the thousands of people who witnessed the spectacle, and the millions more who later read about it, realized that the very first safe elevator had arrived.

It was three more years, however, before developers began to recognize that they could charge a premium for upper floors instead of using them for storage space. It was still another eleven years before passenger elevators were installed in New York office buildings, ushering in the age of the skyscraper and forever changing the way millions of us live and work.

Next time you have a flash of inspiration, don't give up just because everyone else doesn't immediately recognize its value. Stick with it until the rest of the world finally comes around.

One man who understood this principle was Chester F. Carlson, an inventor who wanted to find a way to make better copies. At that time, the only way to make copies was to use a wet, messy, photostatic processes. Carlson was convinced there had to be a better way.

By 1944, Carlson had developed a workable dry-copy technique and, with the help of the Battele Memorial Institute, tried to attract the interest of a manufacturing company with the resources to make the process commercially viable. Reportedly they offered the process to most of the leading companies of the day, including General Electric, IBM, RCA, Kodak, and Bell and Howell. Each in turn rejected the offer.

Carlson and Battele didn't give up. They kept trying to sell the process despite all the rejections. Then one day they received a call from the Haloid Company, a small manufacturer in Rochester, New York. Haloid management had seen a trade journal article on the process and was interested. Eventually an agreement was reached. Soon Carlson's idea, combined with the management talents of Haloid's Joseph C. Wilson Jr., would result in one of the greatest business success stories ever.

Haloid, as you may know, went on to become the huge Xerox Corporation and Carlson's process virtually created a burgeoning multi-billion dollar industry.

When initiative meets persistence, the results can be incredible.

—— POSITIVE ACTION STEPS ——

☞ Don't tell others your great ideas—show them.

☞ You have to believe in yourself and your ideas before you can expect others to believe in you.

☞ Never give up.

DAVE THOMAS— WENDY'S AND WINNING WAYS

Dave Thomas learned the power of positive thinking as a young soldier serving in Germany, and he used it to build the highly successful Wendy's Hamburger chain and a wonderful life for himself and his family.

Dave Thomas was born on July 2, 1932, in Atlantic City, New Jersey, and he very quickly learned about the negative side of life. He never knew his birth parents and his adoptive mother died when he was only five years old.

As a youngster, he moved from state to state as his adoptive father looked for work. "It wasn't easy," Thomas said. "No roots; no sense of belonging. With all that moving, I didn't get a chance to know kids. I guess that's why work became my constant companion."

He began working at the age of twelve, delivering groceries in Knoxville, Tennessee, and was fired in a misunderstanding about the length of his vacation. He landed another job at Walgreens soda fountain but was fired from that job, too, when the boss found out he wasn't sixteen.

Thomas again lied about his age to land another position at a lunch counter. He worked harder than most during his twelve-hour shifts, fearing that he would lose yet another job. "I had been fired twice already," he recalled, "and my father said he would probably have to support me for the rest of my life. He may have been joking, but it made a lasting impression on me."

Thomas saw the seed of an equivalent or greater opportunity in adversity. "My early adversity created a drive in me," he said. "I liked to make money, but money wasn't the only important thing. It was also the sense of accomplishment."

At age eighteen, he joined the Army where he attended cook and baker's school, and soon became one of the youngest soldiers ever to manage an enlisted men's club.

"It was simple," he said. "I just made sure the NCO club was clean, the food was good, and the service fast." It was the same formula he later applied to his restaurant business.

Out of the army, Thomas met the legendary Colonel Harland Sanders when his boss bought a chicken franchise from the Kentucky Colonel. Soon afterward, his boss offered Thomas a deal: take over the management of his struggling Kentucky Fried Chicken carryouts, turn them around, and pay off a $200,000 deficit. If he was successful, Thomas would receive forty-five percent ownership.

Thomas jumped at the chance, despite Colonel Sanders' objections. "The colonel told me not to come over here," he said. "The stores were practically bankrupt; I had four kids and a wife and I was making $135 a week. But I made up my mind that I was going to be in business for myself."

Thomas focused on the stores with intensity. He cut the 100-item menu to mostly chicken and salads and promoted his stores tirelessly, trading buckets of chicken for radio time. He created the familiar bucket of chicken that today adorns KFC restaurants around the world. In 1968, he sold the restaurants back to Kentucky Fried Chicken for $1.5 million.

Thomas founded Wendy's, named after his daughter, the next year. His goals were modest; he hoped someday to have enough restaurants around Columbus, Ohio, to provide summer jobs for his kids.

The imaginative restaurateur pioneered the idea of selling franchises for entire cities and parts of states and the Wendy's concept took off. Since Thomas began franchising his operation two decades ago, Wendy's has grown into a worldwide chain with 7,166 restaurants throughout the U.S. and the world.

Today, the avuncular Thomas is one of the most recognized and admired people in America, thanks in part to his ubiquitous television commercials and his genuine belief that you should put more back into life than you take out. He's active in a number of charities and donates the profits from his autobiography, *Dave's Way* (Berkley Books, New York, 1991), to national adoption awareness campaigns.

The Hortio Alger Award recipient says his recipe for success is hard work, honesty, and total commitment. He says you can create your own opportunities and make a boring job exciting and challenging by finding something that needs to be done and volunteering to do it or by finding the solution to a problem everybody agrees should be solved. "A little initiative will improve your luck nine times out of ten." He says, "You can have anything you want if you set your goals high enough."

—— POSITIVE ACTION STEPS ——

☞ Find something that needs to be
done and volunteer to do it.

☞ Set your goals high. With hard
work you can reach them.

☞ Don't let hardship be an excuse. Dave Thomas
overcame poverty and the loss of his parents at a
young age and became a successful millionaire.

DAY 26

ABSOLUTELY, POSITIVELY— FEDERAL EXPRESS

Federal Express founder and chairman Fred Smith so values leadership ability that in addition to managers giving employees performance evaluations, once a year he turns the tables and lets workers evaluate the bosses.

As a young marine corps officer in Vietnam, Smith was appalled by the lives he saw wasted in sudden death, but he was also discouraged by the lives he saw that would be wasted because the people who managed the workers expected so little from them—and they got it.

Smith, who won six medals for bravery, including a Silver Star and two Purple Hearts during his two tours in Vietnam, learned that powerless people demand only one thing in life, and that thing is respect. When they are treated with respect, they respond with fierce loyalty and dedication. They give their all to leaders who treat them as they deserve to be treated. It's a lesson he never forgot, and it was a major building block of Federal Express.

Smith so believes in the importance of leaders earning the respect of the people they manage and giving respect in return that every spring, Federal Express turns the performance evaluation process upside down. Employees can express their views about their immediate manager as well as all the levels above their supervisor and their opinions about the company as a whole. They are also asked if issues they raised in the previous year's evaluation were handled to their satisfaction. Responses are anonymous, but a summary from people who report directly to them is provided to every manager. Employee ratings on specific leadership attributes are then analyzed to identify any changes the manager needs to make.

But wouldn't this process simply degenerate into a popularity contest with bosses pandering to employees to get good ratings? I posed that question to Jean Ward-Jones, FedEx's manager of quality education and administration. She quickly pointed out that employee ratings are only one element of the evaluation. Managers are also rated on specific, measurable people, service, and profit goals. And they are expected to improve in each area every year.

Fred Smith empowered his employees long before it became a business buzzword and went on to build one of the world's great success stories. He truly believes that ordinary people will do extraordinary things—if they are only given a chance.

To inspire his workers to do their best, Smith rewards workers in a variety of ways. One is the "Bravo Zulu" or BZ award. BZ is the semaphore signal from an aircraft carrier to a pilot to congratulate him or her on a good landing. It's the Marine Corps version of an "attaboy." When a worker receives a BZ on a note or letter from his manager, he knows it's something special. For performance that is over and above that of a simple BZ, managers can request a $25 or $50 check to be sent along with the BZ certificate.

Perhaps the most powerful motivator of all is every employee's right to ask, "What's in it for me?" They don't have to blindly follow some procedure just because someone wrote it down somewhere. They are given the latitude to accomplish the job any way they think best, as long as it gets done. They also can seek redress through a grievance process if they feel they have been treated unfairly. It's appropriately called the "guaranteed fair treatment" procedure, and workers can air any problems they have from performance evaluations to promotions.

If the director cannot work out a solution, it gets bumped up to a vice president. If there's still a problem, there is the board of appeals, which is similar to a supreme court, where the employee and his manager each can have up to three witnesses present information on their behalf.

It's all part of making sure that people in the company feel that they really have a voice and will be heard when there is a problem.

By giving others the respect that they deserve and by empowering them to do the best job they can do, Fred Smith has built Federal Express from a small struggling company into a multi-billion dollar company.

—— POSITIVE ACTION STEPS ——

☞ Respect those from whom you demand respect.

☞ Use incentive programs to give
subordinates a stake in your success.

☞ Reward special efforts with special rewards.

DAY 27

BORROWER TO BILLIONAIRE— CURT CARLSON

How do you start with just $50 in borrowed capital and turn it into one of America's largest privately owned corporations? Curt Carlson says he did it largely by developing what Napoleon Hill called "definiteness of purpose."

Carlson says knowing where he was going and planning how to get there enabled him to build one of America's largest privately held corporations. It also made him one of the country's wealthiest entrepreneurs. Today, Carlson serves as chairman and CEO of Minneapolis-based Carlson Companies, which includes Radisson Hotels International, Colony Hotels & Resorts, TGI Friday's, and a number of other restaurant chains.

"When I started in business," Carlson says, "I wrote my ultimate goal on a little piece of paper, folded it and carried it with me until I reached that goal. Sometimes the paper was frayed and dog-eared by the time I reached my goal, but after I attained it, I wrote down a new goal and carried that paper with me."

Carlson said, "I carried it with me so I would always know it was there. It became part of me. And because it was written, it became crystallized in my mind. It helped clarify my thinking and made it easier to make decisions. When you have a fixed goal, you can quickly evaluate whether your decisions will be toward your goal or away from it."

His first goal when he started his Gold Bond Stamp Company was to earn $100 a week. That little piece of paper, he said, was the flag that drove him on.

Carlson survived the Great Depression and rationing during World War II that virtually eliminated the appeal of trading stamps, but he didn't get his big break until the 1950s when he sold his first supermarket chain. When the consumerist movement of the 1960s shifted the focus to price cutting and away from premiums and promotions, Carlson diversified into the hotel and travel business.

A longtime proponent of a five-year plan. Carlson's goal for his company was to double sales every five years. To do so, every manager's goal was to increase sales by a minimum of fifteen percent annually. Carlson still uses the same simple formula he adopted more than five decades ago. It is:

1. Set a definite timetable for reaching your goal.

2. Never give in to adversity. "Obstacles," Carlson says, "are those frightening things you see when you take your eyes off the target."

3. Go public with your goal—if you keep it to yourself it's too easy to give up.

4. Be realistic. Your goal should be definite and achievable.

Break your goal down into smaller parts that add up to your ultimate goal. For next year, for example, spell out your action plan by months.

Using this formula Carlson has been able to grow his company over the last forty years at an amazing compounded annual rate of thirty-three percent a year.

During the recession of the early '90s, when other travel and hospitality companies were complaining about the economy, Carlson called his executives together and said: "Don't worry about the recession. There is plenty of business out there for us so let's not blame the marketplace for any sales problems."

His managers continued to accomplish great results while the rest of the industry limped along.

The company has always changed with the times and now Carlson is changing his planning methods. In 1992, the company moved to a three-year planning cycle replacing the five-year cycle that Carlson had followed for more than three decades. "I think three years is more realistic going into the Nineties and the year 2000," he told his executives. "We will simply examine our progress more often."

Carlson's goal setting and planning approach, combined with his no-nonsense management style that holds every employee responsible for his or her individual performance, had paid off for Curt Carlson. It will work for you too.

⸺ POSITIVE ACTION STEPS ⸺

☞ Write your goal down and carry it with you.

☞ Break your goal down into manageable steps,
and set a timetable for reaching each.

☞ Evaluate your progress on a regular basis.

DAY 28

MORE THAN COSMETICS— MARY KAY ASH

When she was a young housewife with no sales training or product knowledge, Mary Kay Ash sold ten sets of child psychology books—with the sheer power of her enthusiasm—so she could earn one set for herself.

She has since parlayed that enthusiasm into a multi-million dollar company that operates in nineteen countries around the world. Her name is a household word, and Mary Kay beauty consultants and their ubiquitous pink Cadillacs are an American institution.

Mary Kay Cosmetics was built on two fundamental principles that have guided the company since it was founded more than thirty years ago: First, the organization would be based on the Golden Rule; second, she would build a company that would provide women with an unlimited opportunity for success.

What keeps her going after all she's achieved, she said, is "The young people in our sales force are extremely enthusiastic about their jobs, They believe Mary Kay is the best opportunity in the whole world. It keeps me inspired to do more!"

Ash has also known her share of adversity. As a young salesperson for Stanley Home Products, she borrowed $12 to travel from her home in Dallas to Houston to attend the company's 1937 convention, packing a box of crackers and a pound of cheese because she couldn't afford to eat in restaurants.

It was while she was with Stanley that Ash had one of those days that every salesperson dreads. She awoke on a Monday morning to find that every appointment for the week had canceled. "So, I thought I'd get on the phone and call my Sunday school class. Surely one of them would help me. But, nothing.

"They would say, 'Mary Kay, if that was the last thing on earth, I wouldn't do it.' Stanley parties were not exactly what you would call fun. What woman wants to be told how to wax the floor or clean the wall?

"So I would make a few calls and every few minutes, I would put down the phone and just cry. Then I would get back on the phone and make more calls. Finally, my maid (I had a maid because I didn't want to use dollar time on penny jobs. Besides, no man scrubs floors before he goes to work!) after listening to me for an hour came in and said, 'Miss Mary Kay, I'll have a Stanley party for you.'

"So I went to her home and found she had invited some very nice people and I couldn't beat them off with a fly swatter. Most of them were in the maid business, and they had never seen these products before. They were very interested in what I had to say."

Soon afterward, Ash had a black sales unit, and her team rocketed to the top. She battled prejudiced neighbors who petitioned to keep her from inviting blacks to her home during the dark days of segregation, determined to treat them with the courtesy and respect she gave to all of her customers and sales associates.

Ash left Stanley after eleven years of service when her male assistant, whom she trained, was made her boss at twice her salary. When the company ignored her protests, she left to start her own company.

She and her late husband invested their life savings of $5,000 in her "dream company," which would offer women unprecedented opportunities for financial independence, career advancement, and personal fulfillment. She wouldn't limit them as she had been; she would encourage them to reach their true potential.

A month before the 500-square-foot store was to open, her husband dropped dead of a heart attack at the breakfast table. She was forty-five years old and terrified, but with the help of her twenty-year-old son, Richard (now chairman of the company) and eight salespeople, she went ahead.

Today, the chairman emeritus of Mary Kay Cosmetics, Ash is the only female chairman of a Fortune 500 company; her net worth is estimated at about $320 million; and her company has been named one of the "100 best companies to work for in America."

In her book, *Mary Kay on People Management* (Warner Books, 1984), Ash advises: Always tell your employees the truth. If you don't know the answer to something, say so. Most people recognize a smoke screen when they see one. If your employees ask something you cannot reveal, tell them. They will understand.

She also says, be consistent in both facts and attitude. Consistency will help your employees better understand you, and it will make them more secure in their jobs. Be relaxed and confident in your dealings with others. Think things through before you speak, say what you mean and be yourself. She adds, use "we" instead of "I" when you talk about your people to others. Word will definitely get around that you respect their contributions.

And finally, Ash warns that you must remember where you came from. Your future in management depends upon your ability to work well with others. Arrogance and pomposity are not admirable qualities—especially in a manager.

—— POSITIVE ACTION STEPS ——

☞ Use the power of enthusiasm to help
you accomplish your goals.

☞ Adopt the Golden Rule in your business dealings: "Do
unto others as you would have them do unto you."

☞ Believe in yourself. Others will follow.

CHAPTER FIVE

PUTTING TEAMWORK TO WORK

Working with others will allow you to accomplish far more than you can possibly achieve alone. This chapter includes articles on how to work with, for, and lead others.

DAY 29

MORE THAN MONEY

Are you being paid what you're really worth? If your answer is "no," you must somehow prove to your employer that you are indeed worth more.

It is well known that those who achieve great success in life are those people who give more than is expected of them. They go the extra mile. They prove to their superiors they are worth more, instead of waiting to be paid more before they improve their performance. They become indispensable to their bosses or their clients and customers because they can always be counted upon. They are there when they are needed, and they collect rewards commensurate with their efforts.

Napoleon Hill developed a formula for this process. Stated simply, it says that the quality of service rendered, plus the quantity of service rendered, plus the mental attitude in which it is rendered, equals your compensation in the world and the amount of space you will occupy in the hearts of your fellow man.

Going the extra mile also provides additional benefits. It makes you more proficient at what you do. And because you can be counted on to give more than expected, your boss, customers, or clients will give you better opportunities and more responsibility.

You will also find you like yourself better and so will your friends, family, and co-workers. It is hard to dislike one who always works harder, runs faster, jumps higher, and digs deeper than everyone else. And because you know how much more you have to do, you will be less inclined to procrastinate. You will become a person of action, one others recognize as an individual who "gets things done."

Once you've gone the extra mile and found out that it really is the key to success, you may find your horizons expanding, that you now feel capable of doing things you only dreamed of before.

Many people have left mundane occupations to pursue their dreams. Sean Connery started out as a truck driver and bricklayer. Boxer George Forman worked as an electronics assembler. Israeli Prime Minister Golda Meir began as a schoolteacher.

It doesn't matter what you do or what you wish to do. To achieve success and to be paid what you are really worth, you have to always go that extra mile. The world is filled with competent people. What the world truly needs and is willing to pay dearly for are people who excel.

If you're on the other side of the fence, a business owner or manager, you may find that in today's intensely competitive world, it's increasingly harder to find the money to give good raises to good workers. Fortunately, few of us are motivated by money alone.

Following are some actions you can take to show your employees that you care about them and that you value their contributions.

Give better performers a title. It costs nothing and lets the employee know that you recognize he or she is performing at a high level.

Be generous with business cards. They are relatively inexpensive but are great builders of self-esteem.

Redesign the office space to treat everyone a little more equally. Nothing erects barriers between the "haves" and "have nots" like offices. Consider having smaller offices supplemented by common conference or meeting areas.

Give awards generously. Plaques, certificates, even "atta-boy" stickers help keep workers motivated. We all like to know that our hard work is recognized and that we are appreciated for our contributions.

Ensure that every individual in the organization is treated with the kind of respect that you expect from them. Respect your people and they will perform miracles for you. Of course, you must make sure you are worthy of your employees' respect in both word and deed. A good officer always makes sure the troops are cared for before attending to his or her own personal wants and needs. It's a good system to follow in any line of work.

Make sure you are being impeccably fair. Nothing destroys individual incentive like the belief that the only people who get ahead are the boss' pals. It also helps if, in hiring, you don't hire anyone who you wouldn't want to work for yourself. If you aren't compatible with them, chances are good that your employees won't like working with them either.

Of course, sooner or later, there will come a time to give raises. When it comes time to loosen the purse strings, link pay with performance. Design a reward system based on what people accomplish rather than on how many hours they work. Above all, follow the Golden Rule in your dealings with employees. If you treat them as you would like to be treated, they will reward you with loyalty, devotion, and exceptional performance.

POSITIVE ACTION STEPS

☞ Reward achievers with recognition
in addition to money.

☞ Retain and motivate key employees.

☞ Make it a habit to go the extra mile.

DAY 30

NETWORKING

Maintaining your network is still the best way to keep your job or find a new one as companies cut back, lay off, and reorganize to more effectively compete in today's global economy.

It's too late for you to begin your job search after the ax has fallen, according to executive search consultant Don Dvorak. "What you should have been doing all along is developing visibility for yourself because you already have the beginnings of your network in place," Dvorak said.

He also advises: Keep up with what's going on in your industry, your business, or your profession, and make sure that you help others along the way—because you never know when you might need some assistance yourself. And you never know what source help may come from.

When Merrilee, my wife, and I were first married, I was "between engagements" as it were, supporting myself as a freelance writer while I looked for another job. One day, I got a call from a friend I had met at a journalism society meeting, inviting me to lunch. I hadn't seen him for over a year, but his wife, whom I had never met, saw my wedding picture in the newspaper and remembered her husband mentioning my name on occasion.

Over lunch, he told me about an open position at his company that matched my background and experience. He introduced me to the right people, and in a matter of days I was on the payroll.

If your personal job search plan included this bizarre set of circumstances, any rational person would think you're crazy. But that's the way networking works. A friend of a friend hears about an opportunity, and eventually something works out. It's also true that there's a lot of timing and luck involved. There are always more ambitious, motivated people than there are good jobs. You just have to find the right set of circumstances when the conditions are right for you.

You can help make sure that you are in the right place at the right time by creating plenty of opportunities for the right circumstances to come together. You can't manage events, but you can manage your reaction to them. When you fail at something through no fault of your own, you can accept defeat and give up, or you can learn from the experience and refocus your energies in a direction that will ultimately lead to success. Perhaps Texas Longhorn Coach Darrell Royal put it best. He said, "Luck is what happens when preparation meets opportunity."

Part of that preparation is to keep a positive attitude, no matter what happens. It really does make a difference, as the following story demonstrates.

Alan Schaffer is an attorney who specializes in bankruptcy litigation. He's bright, he's motivated, and he's a very hard worker. During his years on the job, he has consistently received high praise from his clients, his peers, and the partners in the firm. He was on the fast track to the partnership himself when suddenly his world was turned upside down.

An expanding economy reduced the number of bankruptcy filings, and his firm lost a big client. There wasn't enough work to support the attorneys in the bankruptcy practice, so the managing partner was forced to notify them that their employment would be terminated in a matter of weeks. Instead of being devastated, Schaffer was philosophical. "Those things happen," he said, and he started looking for another job.

Along with many of his other friends and associates, he sent copies of his resume to contacts in law firms telling them, "This is a good guy; you should look at him if you have any openings."

He worked all the contacts and kept his friends informed of his progress, but nothing worked out. The other firms had the same problem—not enough work to support another attorney.

All the time he searched for a new position, Schaffer still went to work early and stayed late, prepared his cases for court, and worked just as hard as he ever had.

Occasionally when I ran into him, I would ask him how things were going and he would say, "Well they gave me some new cases. I don't know if that means they are thinking about keeping me or if one day they will ask me, 'What are you doing still here? I thought you were gone.'"

But he wouldn't let the situation get him down. He was determined to do his best until his last day on the job. He continued to do his best until everyone else in the practice was gone. He was the only bankruptcy attorney left.

A week later, he got the word. The firm was going to keep him. He was too valuable to lose. Whether you have a job or are looking for one, the old rule still applies: The only difference between winners and losers is *their attitude.*

—— POSITIVE ACTION STEPS ——

☞ Call an old colleague and catch up with what's new. Renewing ties strengthens your network.

☞ Tell everyone you know, even those not in your field, that you are looking for a job. They may know somebody who knows somebody.

☞ Above all, keep a positive mental attitude.

DAY 31

HELPING OTHERS HELPS YOU

We've all met successful people who claim they are self-made. But as Napoleon Hill once pointed out, people who claim that they are "self-made" only prove that it's possible for ingrates to make money.

Hill learned early that every person who reaches the top receives substantial boosts along the way from others. He, himself, reached a turning point when the wealthy capitalist Andrew Carnegie advised him to begin organizing the "Science of Success" as a definitive philosophy and gave him active help and support to do so.

Later, Hill hoped that in passing on what he learned through his lifetime of research, he would pay off the debt incurred when Carnegie lent him aid so many decades ago. Hill reasoned that the simple law of fair play requires that we respond by helping others just the way we have been helped.

You can actually further your own career by helping others achieve their goals. As Hill says, there is no greater truth than the wonderful epigram: "Help thy brother's boat across and lo! thine own hath reached the shore."

He points out that no man is more wealthy than the one who has the time and energy to spend in helping others. Notice, he didn't mention money. Money is fine, too, for helping others, but time and effort are even more precious. That's because the pay-off in satisfaction and self-contentment is commensurate with the investment.

One of the richest experiences you'll ever enjoy is to be able to point to someone at their peak of success and say, "I helped put him there," Hill said.

Your efforts on behalf of someone less fortunate may not only help him or her, they may also add something of priceless value to your soul—regardless of whether he or she recognizes your aid or is even grateful for it.

As Hill wrote, "Think how the world would be transformed if each of us 'adopted' someone else to help through life! In turn, each of us would be adopted and receive help."

In today's busy world, we seldom take the time to lend a hand to those who would benefit most from our help. That's too bad, because when we miss out on those opportunities, we also miss out on a great opportunity to help ourselves.

Nowhere is this principle more sorely lacking than on the job. We all know that people respond to positive encouragement, yet a lot of people seem to forget everything they know about how to treat other people when they become the boss.

When you're in charge and you're trying to get something accomplished, it's easy to forget the way other people feel. Some folks become so intent on their own objectives that they forget about others, or worse, instead of encouraging their employees, they threaten them. Fear may be a great short-term motivator, but intimidation will not win the hearts and souls of your people and persuade them to do what's necessary to achieve lasting success.

The real measure of a leader is how well you look after your people. If you want them to take care of you, you have to take care of them. You need them to help you accomplish your mission, and you must give them reasons to give you the cheerful and enthusiastic support that you need to achieve great things. You have to give them reasons to align their goals with yours—reasons that are sincere, logical, and persuasive.

The best leaders I know are those whose people know that they really care about them. They take the time and trouble to learn about their goals and dreams and aspirations, and they ask about their families. When their people have problems, good leaders listen and offer help. They show their people every day by their behavior that they care about them. They also know that every individual in every job is important.

Not long ago, I was in a late meeting with the CEO of a major public company when the janitor came in to clean the conference room. The boss greeted him by name, and stopped the meeting so he could take away the trash and the empty coffee cups. When I commented on his consideration, he said, "I'm not just being kind. That guy's important. From his point of view, he's the only one here who is working. The rest of us are just sitting around talking. And if you don't think he's important, try getting along without him. If he doesn't show up some day, you may find that he's the most important guy in the company."

In my view, that's a real leader.

—— POSITIVE ACTION STEPS ——

☞ Make a list of people who might need your help.

    ☞ Make a list of the abilities and resources
you have that can benefit others.

☞ Try to help at least one person a day. Start today.

OFFICE POLITICS

I t's not easy for CEOs to make the tough decisions necessary to effectively compete in the world today, but it may be a whole lot tougher on everyone else than the boss thinks.

Business periodicals and books these days are filled with strategies for downsizing, right-sizing, restructuring, or refocusing on your core business. There's no doubt you've got to be good. And it's not enough to be as good as any company in your industry— you've got to be as good as any company in any business. Your customers are a reflection of all their experiences—good and bad. They are going to compare your quality, price, and service to every company with which they have ever done business.

As you think about how you are going to consolidate your operations and improve productivity, don't forget that whatever business you are in, people are still your greatest asset. You can install the most modern equipment and adopt the most efficient operating practices in the world, but you still need good people to make it work.

As you ask your people to do more and more work and you lay off workers in efficiency moves, you might want to recall the words of the London School of Business' Dr. Gary Hamel. He cautions managers to remember that restructuring and re-engineering should not be construed to be innovation. Such consolidation moves are the things managers do to pay for their sins of the past. It's also important to remember, he says, that "the first rats off the ship will be the best swimmers."

Your best people won't wait around for the second or third rounds of cuts. They will be working for your competitors. Good managers recognize this and they create opportunities for growth and development as they take the painful steps to prepare the business to compete in the years ahead.

If you are consolidating or refocusing your company, your department, or your business, make sure your re-engineering plans include a strategy for taking care of your best people.

How you treat the employees you must eliminate says a lot to the people left behind. And the old expression that "those who live by the sword die by the sword" is especially appropriate. How you treat people you are forced to terminate is a good barometer of how you will be treated if you ever find yourself on the other side of the desk. If you work for a company that tends to view people as expendable, the chances are good that someday you will probably be fired—regardless of how valuable you perceive yourself to be.

Treating others fairly when you terminate them may help ensure that you get fair treatment when your time comes. Even if you own the company and you may never be fired yourself, there are some things that you should consider when you are thinking about terminating someone.

First, in addition to laws that require fair and equitable treatment, how you treat people will make a tremendous impression on those who remain in your organization.

Regardless of their performance, it's natural for the employees to identify with the worker. Any firing generates a degree of insecurity among workers. If they believe that you treated those affected fairly, they will be more likely to see the situation favorably and believe that you will be fair to them when they make mistakes.

You can be sure that your competitors will make as much of the situation as they can, as well. They may tell your customers that because you are cutting your staff, you can't provide the same level of service that they can, or that you can't keep good people because you are too difficult to work for. And you can be sure that word will get around in your industry.

I once worked for a firm that cut a very small percentage of its staff during a recession, and according to our own surveys, it was five years before prospective recruits began to believe that we were as stable as our competitors.

How compassionately you treat workers whom you have to fire is important to them and it's important to you, but it's especially important to those who remain, workers whose performance is critical to your success.

—— POSITIVE ACTION STEPS ——

☞ Share the credit with co-workers.

☞ Do favors for co-workers before they can ask for it.

☞ Compliment co-workers on their achievements.

DAY 33

ORDINARY PEOPLE DO EXTRAORDINARY THINGS

The trouble with cows, an old farmer once observed, is that they don't stay milked. The same is true with keeping a commitment. It is not something that is done once and forgotten. Changing your life requires reaffirmation of your commitment until it becomes a habit.

Most of us start out with the best of intentions (often around January 1st of each year), planning the improvements we wish to make in our habits and our lives. Then, reality gradually sets in, and we remember why we do things the way we do. It is easier, it is pleasurable, or it is part of a lifestyle developed over a long period of time.

Eliminating bad habits and replacing them with good ones requires discipline and determination. Make it a practice to reaffirm your goal every day until it becomes a part of you.

For years, Curtis L. Carlson, founder and chairman of the multi-billion dollar Carlson Companies, wrote down his goal on a little piece of paper and carried it in his wallet. Each day, he would take the paper out of his wallet and reread it and renew his commitment to achieving his goal. The constant reinforcement helped him to create a fortune.

W. Clement Stone suggests repeating your goal aloud several times in the morning and evening. If you repeat something often enough, your mind will accept it as fact and help you transform your goal into physical reality.

Visualization also helps reinforce your commitment. Imagine yourself getting in your new automobile. Picture yourself unlocking the front door of the dream house you have just purchased. Think of what you will say when you congratulate your son or daughter upon graduation from a prestigious university. Post in a prominent place a photo of the car or house you desire or the campus of the university to which you plan to send your children. Look at it every day and reaffirm your commitment to achieving your goal.

There are few things in life that you cannot have if you set your mind on them, develop a workable plan, take the necessary action steps, and follow through with determination and dedication.

Far too many people look for reasons to fail instead of focusing on what is possible for them to achieve. So when you begin to doubt that it is possible for you to achieve great success, think about the following people and what they had to overcome.

Ludwig Van Beethoven was deaf. By the time he reached his early thirties hearing was difficult for him; by age forty-six, he was completely deaf. Yet he wrote his greatest music during his later years.

Sarah Bernhardt—the divine Sarah, regarded by many as the greatest actress France has ever produced—had her leg amputated as a result of an injury. She continued to star on the stage until just prior to her death at the age of seventy-nine.

Louis Braille was blinded at age three. He became a teacher and developed the Braille system for the blind.

Miguel De Cervantes lost his arm in battle and lived in poverty most of his life. *Don Quixote* and his other works have arguably made him Spain's most prominent literary figure.

Helen Keller was blind and deaf by age two, yet became one of America's best-known people. A hugely successful lecturer and author, she wrote ten books and many other works.

Franklin Roosevelt taught his countrymen that "we have nothing to fear but fear itself" during the height of the Great Depression. He was paralyzed by polio at age thirty-nine, but went on to become one of America's most beloved leaders. He was elected president four times.

Dr. Henry Viscardi, Jr. was born without legs but served as a Red Cross field officer during World War II. He is president of the Human Resources Center, founder of Abilities, Inc., has thirteen honorary degrees, and has written nine books. He has served as an adviser to several presidents on handicapped issues.

As the lives of these great achievers vividly illustrate, there really are no limits to what you can achieve with your life—except the limitations you place upon yourself.

——— POSITIVE ACTION STEPS ———

☞ Eliminate bad habits by replacing
them with good habits.

☞ Every day visualize yourself achieving
your ultimate goal.

☞ Remember that most great people have
overcome great obstacles to achieve success.

DAY 34

TEAMWORK

One of the hardest lessons for many of us to learn is how to work with a team and to delegate. But the fact is, no matter how good we are or how much better we think we can do something than anyone else, we are limited as to how much we can accomplish by ourselves. However, if we learn to delegate properly, there's no limit to what we can accomplish.

Delegation is an acquired art. We begin our careers as "doers" responsible for performing a job or completing a project ourselves. As a result, we develop a style of doing things that we believe is correct, and we have trouble accepting the fact that there are many ways to do the same thing.

It's natural to believe that we can do the job better than anyone else. The problem is that as you are promoted to higher levels, you have less and less time to perform actual "work." Your time is taken up in planning, in meetings, in administration, and in providing guidance to your team of employees.

Unless you learn to delegate effectively, your effectiveness will decrease drastically. You will eventually reach the point where it is not possible for you to do—or even check—all your employees' work. You have to hire good people, rely on them to do the job right, and create an atmosphere of mutual trust where they can feel free to come to you with problems—not for an answer, but for a discussion of the alternatives.

Your wisdom and experience should be useful to them as a decision-making aid, not for making the decision itself. If you solve all of their problems for them, you deprive them of the opportunity to grow and mature as managers. Naturally, there will be questions of policy, large expenditures, and the like that require your approval as a manager, but if you encourage employees to come to you with recommendations rather than questions, you encourage them to think for themselves—and you allocate your time better as well. If they have thought through the alternatives, you can reach a decision quickly and not waste your time exploring approaches to problems they should have developed.

One manager I know always responds the same way when people come to him with problems. "I'm not interested in problems," he says, "I'm interested in solutions."

However, there are still a lot of people in the world who are much more interested in the process of work than in the results they achieve. They don't realize that at the end of the day, results are all that really matter.

A number of years ago, I worked for a trade association composed of a group of specialists in a profession I won't mention in order to protect the guilty. I was new with the organization when one of my people came to me with a requisition to buy some filing cabinets. When I asked what they were for, she said, "I dunno. Shirley needs them." So I went to see Shirley and asked her. "For the biography files," she said.

"What are the biographies used for?" I asked.

"I don't know," she said. "They send them to me and I'm supposed to file them. I think they are for the public relations department."

So I went to see the PR director. "Are these biography forms yours?" I asked.

"Nope," he said. "We don't use 'em. They're too old. When we write a press release about one of our members, we always ask them for an updated biography. I think the membership department handles them."

So I went to see the membership director. "Yep," she said. "They're ours."

"What do you use them for?" I asked.

"We don't," she said. "The PR department uses them to write press releases about members."

When I told her about my conversation with the PR director, she said, "Well, you'd better talk to Shirley. She handles those things."

So I went back to see Shirley. "Does anyone use these biographical forms?" I asked.

"I couldn't say for sure," she said. "I've only been here five years."

As we were talking, the print shop manager strolled up to tell me that he couldn't print the rush job I had requested because there was a big job ahead of me. "What is it?" I asked.

"We're printing 20,000 biographical data forms for the new membership packets," he said.

We were printing forms by the thousands, mailing them out to members who took the time to fill them out, put them in a postage-paid envelope, and send them back. We opened the envelopes and sent them to Shirley who filed them. Everyone on the team did exactly what they were instructed to do, but it didn't count for anything. We were making something nobody wanted.

I'd venture to say this experience is repeated a thousand times a day in America wherever people care more about the process than the results.

—— POSITIVE ACTION STEPS ——

☞ Find out how the job you do fits into the rest of the organization.

☞ Learn to delegate. Ask for recommendations instead of solving problems for your employees. Let them learn and grow.

☞ Surround yourself with good people, and you will be more confident when it comes time to delegate.

DAY 35

A LITTLE RESPECT

I t's amazing what you can accomplish as a manager if you can learn to control your ego and think about the needs of your employees. Following is the story of one executive who inspires people to highest levels of performance because he respects them.

Not long ago, I attended an early morning meeting with a fellow I know who is the president of a Fortune 500 manufacturing company. He's enormously successful and has thousands of people working for him, but in meetings, he's the guy who pours the coffee for others—he doesn't expect to be treated like royalty. He also answers his own phone. I know that in some circles it's fashionable these days for a CEO to pick up his own phone occasionally to let the little people know he's a regular guy too, but this fellow does it on a regular basis. His friends and associates know that if they need to reach him, they can always find him in the office early in the morning—he starts work about 6:30 a.m.—and if he's in, he picks up the phone.

On this particular day, though, he surprised me yet again with his unfailing courtesy and respect for others. When the phone rang at his secretary's desk, he walked over and answered her phone. Not only did he answer the call, he took a message for her, explaining to the caller that she wasn't in yet. This was obviously not the first time he'd done so, because he knew where she kept the message pad and how to fill out the message form promptly and efficiently. As he politely took the message, I couldn't help but wonder what the caller would think if he or she knew that it was the big boss of the company on the line.

Does this kind of behavior impress others? Well, I can tell you that it certainly impressed me. In my line of work I've had the opportunity to meet a lot of wealthy and famous people and this was the very first time I'd ever seen the president of a Fortune 500 company take a message for his secretary. It certainly hasn't diminished the respect his people have for him either. His consideration for others has made his employees tremendously loyal to him.

When he took over the company, it was losing money and some industry analysts speculated openly about whether the company would declare bankruptcy. A couple of years later, the company is not only in the black, it is was well on its way to record earnings, and its common stock is one of the best performers in its industry.

A little respect for others can pay big dividends.

Another executive I know promoted a couple of people from division vice presidents to group presidents with responsibility for several operating divisions. This is not big news, of course. Promotions like this take place every day in corporate America. What impressed me, though, was the way he handled the promotions.

They would have been perfectly happy if he had called them into his office, told them the good news, given them a firm handshake and a big smile, and sent them on their way. But he didn't do it that way at all.

He waited until a regularly scheduled meeting of all division operating executives, called them up to the podium, and made the announcement. He'd even gone to the trouble to have business cards printed up with their new titles. Do you think those guys are going to be supportive of their boss? You can't buy that kind of loyalty with money. It can come only from the heart.

Another guy I know, when his company signed a million dollar advertising contract with a magazine publisher, knew that the agreement called for half of the amount to be paid up front and the balance to be paid at the end of the term. He could have waited for an invoice and handled it through normal channels, but he didn't. He had a check issued for $500,000 and took it to the celebratory luncheon where the contract would be signed. As soon as the papers were inked, he presented the check to the ad salesman—while all of the salesman's bosses looked on.

When there is a choice of preferential placement of advertising, what company do you think will be top of mind at the magazine? We all know there's a right way and a wrong way to do things, but when you do the right thing with style, grace, and a little respect you make a lasting impression on those who are important to you, and you buy a whole lot more for your money.

—— POSITIVE ACTION STEPS ——

☛ Treat everyone in the company, those below you as well as those above, with common courtesy.

☛ Set a good example for others. Behave as you would want everyone else in the company to act.

☛ Make sure you are worthy of others' respect in all you do.

CHAPTER SIX

SUCCESS AND THE SUBCONSCIOUS

One of the most powerful forces in the universe is the subconscious mind. Once set on a goal, it will subtly guide all actions toward achieving that goal. This week focuses on how to make your subconscious work for you.

DAY 36

COSMIC HABIT FORCE
AND RED CARS

apoleon Hill coined the term "cosmic habit force" to describe the ability of the subconscious mind to transform your thoughts into action. He believed that if you set a goal for yourself, visualize yourself as having achieved it, and continually reinforce the message to your subconscious, it will work around the clock to help you find a way to reach it.

The tough thing about some goals, however, like losing weight or saving for a luxury item, is that it takes so long to achieve them. How do you maintain your enthusiasm?

One schoolteacher I know uses the principle of continual reinforcement in a simple, innocuous way to get anything she wants. She simply posts a picture of the things she desires on the refrigerator door with little magnets. Several times a day, when she sees the object of her desire, it reinforces the message, not only in her mind, but in the mind of her family.

When she wanted a new, red sports car, she put a picture of her face over the model who appeared in the advertisement. Her family and friends snickered, but every time she passed the refrigerator, she saw herself at the wheel of that sports car. Although the cost of the car was beyond her means, the burning desire she created in herself to own the car motivated her to make extra money in a part-time direct-selling job and to cut expenses.

Within six months from the time she posted the picture of the car on the refrigerator door, she owned it. It wasn't just a fluke. She went on to buy the house she wanted using the same system. It took a little longer, of course, but she eventually succeeded.

The family, no longer doubters, even helped work at saving money. Before long they were living in that house.

You can do the same thing, Set your goals, constantly and consistently reinforce the message, and the cosmic habit force will help make it happen. The secret is to never give up, especially when the going gets tough. An example of a person who found the importance of such a commitment in the face of adversity is Bill Clement.

As a hockey player, Clement played on two championship teams with the Philadelphia Flyers. When he retired from hockey, he quickly went broke in the restaurant business, but he didn't give up.

Clement says that almost everyone passes through what he calls the "red zone" at one time or another. The red zone is the point where adversity becomes so great that those who are not committed to being the best resign themselves to defeat, being second, or even worse, they quit. It's the make or break point.

The term *red zone* was borrowed from another sport—football. In football, the area from the twenty-yard line to the goal is called the red zone. It is the toughest part of the field to move the ball, but if you don't get through the red zone, you won't get any touchdowns.

Clement spent some time in the red zone after he lost his money in the restaurant business. He decided he'd better get in touch with who he is and what he stands for to see if he has what it takes to make it. He calls it his commitment. It is:

1. I will be honest and sincere with my audience and listeners.

2. I will not allow my ego or my temper to overrule my head in a decision.

3. I am a leader. My positive attitude during difficult times will reflect this.

4. I will try to be gentle, objective, and fair with my wife and my kids.

5. When someone engages my services, I will always give them more than they pay for.

6. I am not the toughest guy in the world, but I will never quit.

Clement says, "It's easy to score when nothing or no one is trying to stop you, but you have to be the best when the competition gets tougher. How you react to adversity will determine whether or not you are going to be the best."

—— POSITIVE ACTION STEPS ——

☞ Visualize yourself attaining your
goal several times each day.

☞ Post pictures of your goal where
you will see them every day.

☞ Total commitment to your goal will get
you through the "red zones" of life.

DAY 37

THE IMPORTANCE OF SOLITUDE

Although we need to cultivate positive lasting relationships with others, we still need time to ourselves. In solitude we can better hear ourselves and determine what it is that we truly want from life.

Early in his career, Napoleon Hill wrote: "I love my family and friends deeply. But I also love to get away from the crowds, away from everybody and visit with myself. This may seem rather selfish, but it isn't. My mental health demands it."

Hill went on to say that he loved to think, to look ahead and anticipate the experiences yet to come in his life, to figure out why he was put on this earth and what to do to fulfill his mission in life. He loved to go just a step further in imagination than he ever went in realization. In other words, he loved to daydream.

Contrary to what some may believe, dreaming is not harmful. In fact, quite the opposite is true. Getting away from others to dream allows you to rise above commonplace thoughts and things. Milton did his best work after blindness forced him to turn to solitude for realization. Francis Scott Key wrote "The Star-Spangled Banner" while being held as a prisoner of war on a British ship.

When we are with others, we must be polite and discuss with them whatever subject they may happen to bring up. When we are with ourselves, we can direct our thoughts along any line we choose and concentrate upon those thoughts, impress them upon our minds, and keep them where we can retrieve them when we want them.

Nowadays, we call it visualization, but it is really nothing more than constructive dreaming!

No one ever becomes a doer without first becoming a dreamer. The architect first draws a picture of a building in his mind and then places it on paper. The great scientist Albert Einstein said that he really understood the theory of relativity only after he visualized himself riding a beam of light through space. When he imagined what would happen when he rode the beam, he was then able to work out the mathematical formulas that proved the theory.

Dreams also can reveal to us those things we want most out of life. In essence, dreaming can help us create our "wish list." Wishes, like dreams, take up no room, they have no weight, and if they are not acted upon, they are of no real value. But if you are committed to your wishes and put in the required effort, there is practically no wish that you can't make come true.

The first step, of course, is determining which wish to act upon. Each of us is able to generate more wishes than we could possibly fulfill in a lifetime, so we must first isolate that one wish above all others that we would like to make reality.

A good exercise is to write down all your wishes. Don't limit yourself; act as if each wish were possible—because at this point they are. After you get them all on paper, rank them in order of importance to you. You may even find that some wishes are merely stepping stones to a greater wish. Having your wish list written down where you can see it clearly will make the task of choosing between wishes a lot easier.

The next step is to set up a plan of action. Decide what steps you can take to get you on your way toward realizing your goal. Don't be discouraged by the fact that there may be a long way to go before you reach your ultimate goal. Just keep in mind the sooner you get started, the sooner you will arrive.

It is also true that just having your wish clearly in mind makes the job easier. That's because we all tend to subconsciously act to make our desires come true. It's a self-fulfilling prophecy. If you believe you will fail in a task, you will. On the other hand, if you are certain you can attain your wish, your subconscious will help guide your every action toward making it happen.

Of course, you will encounter obstacles that must be overcome. However, when you concentrate upon a wish that you really want to make come true, you will discover that your mind will work overtime to find alternate ways to achieve your goal. After all, usually there are many paths to the same objective.

As you work toward your goal, don't be discouraged by people who will tell you why your wish can't come true. They may simply be envious. Whatever the reason, never let anyone steal your wish.

People ridiculed the Wright brothers when they wished to fly like a bird; educated men thought Edison was wasting his time trying to conquer darkness; and skeptics scoffed at Henry Ford's dream to make the automobile affordable to the masses.

Wishes do come true—if they are supported by a burning desire, a good plan, and the hard work and determination necessary to make it happen.

—— POSITIVE ACTION STEPS ——

☞ Use quiet time to focus on solutions
to problems and setbacks.

☞ Let daydreams point the way to
what you want most in life.

☞ Write down all your wishes as though each
can come true. Then focus on the one or
two most important wishes. You can make
them come true if you're committed.

DAY 38

HABIT FORCE

H ave you ever done something automatically then attributed it to "force of habit"? You can use that same compelling force, the force of habit, to help you achieve your goals.

Our universe thrives on order and despises chaos. As scientists learn more about the composition of our universe, they find that though everything is in a state of change, it is in a state of orderly change. Nowhere is this process more readily apparent than in nature. All plants and animals go through an organized process of change, from birth through growth, maturity, and death.

Just as nature uses repetitive patterns to bring order out of chaos, so do we. To simplify our lives, we form habits. We do things a certain way, without even thinking, and for no reason other than we have always done them that way. We shave our faces or put on makeup in the same order because when were first learning how, we got in the habit of doing things that way. It is a useful tool to simplify our lives because we no longer have to think in great detail about everything we do.

Of course, habits themselves make no moral judgments; they can either be good or bad. Both are formed in the same way: through repetition. We try something, we like it, and we keep doing it—probably the exact same way each time. But the one thing that sets mankind apart in the grand scheme of things is that we can decide what habits we would like to develop.

We can use to our advantage the knowledge that habits are formed through repetition and reinforcement. By deciding which habits we would like to develop, we can condition ourselves to change our behavior and become the people we would like to be.

You can replace bad habits with good ones through repetition and reinforcement. You can replace negative thoughts with positive ones, you can replace inaction with action; you can form any habit you choose. Of course, I don't mean to imply that changing habits is easy. You have to work on it over time, like alcoholics who give up drinking one drink at a time and dieters who lose weight one pound at a time. But you can do it.

If you want to train yourself to do an unpleasant job right away instead of procrastinating, for example, force yourself to do it right away once, then once again, and continue the same pattern until you no longer think about it, you just do it automatically. If you want to eat carrots instead of Twinkies, you do it a carrot at a time and a Twinkie at a time. Work on your new habit one day at a time, and soon tomorrow will take care of itself.

—— POSITIVE ACTION STEPS ——

☞ Write down the bad habits you want to replace.

☞ Next to the bad habits you plan to replace, write the good habits you would like to adopt.

☞ Focus on doing the good habit you wish to establish just for today. Tomorrow do the same. Soon it's a firmly established habit.

DAY 39

CONTROLLED ATTENTION

No one ever achieved great success without focus. When you totally focus on a goal, your subconscious mind automatically causes you to tailor your every action toward the fulfillment of that goal. Self-fulfilling prophecies are manifestations of controlled attention. When you truly believe something will happen, you may subconsciously take action to bring about that outcome.

You can use the power of controlled attention to your benefit. Begin by writing down your goal. This will force you to develop an objective that is crystal clear. Take your written goal with you wherever you go, and read it several times a day.

At the end of each day before you sleep, recall your goal and everything you have done that day to move closer to it. If you find your actions are taking away from your goal, try to determine why, and readjust your actions.

The difference between highly successful people and aimless, unhappy people is that successful people set high goals for themselves, they form the habit of doing the things that are necessary to achieve their goals, and they fill their minds with positive thoughts. Unsuccessful people simply drift, letting negative influences dominate their minds. Eventually negativity fills their lives.

You become what you think about most. Concentrate on positive influences and goals and you will attain a positive, fulfilling life. Concentrate on negative influences and bad things happen.

The incredible power of concentration can sometimes be demonstrated in some very strange and unexpected ways. A few years ago, Paul Zuromski, publisher of *Psychic Guide*, a magazine that explores parapsychological phenomena in an attempt to facilitate "understanding and improving body, mind and spirit," conducted a highly unusual test.

Charmed by the so-called psychokinetic metal bending of Uri Geller in the 1970s, and others who followed, Zuromski decided to test the possibilities on a psychic development class. He said, "I figured that because these people are in tune with what I was trying to do, twisting the spoons would be simple."

Of course, it turned out to be a bit more complicated. His first experiment ended in failure. He consulted with a friend more experienced in such matters, who helped him refine the procedure, and tried again, this time with a group of eighteen people. Again nothing happened.

He wrote in his magazine, "I began to see my future as a spoon-bending facilitator twist and turn away."

Then one woman yelled. She was holding the spoon upright by the tip of the handle. Her spoon had fallen over by itself—it bent where the bowl meets the handle. Then most everyone else's spoon started bending. In fact, about fifteen of the eighteen people there bent their spoons to some degree.

Evidently, they needed to see a spoon bend to give their own belief system the proof it needed to transcend the ingrained, "I can't do this" to "I can." The "can't" became invalid because of what their eyes had seen.

Whether or not you believe the account of Zuromski and his eighteen witnesses—indeed, you may write it off to group hypnosis or some sort of a magic trick—is beside the point.

Zuromski asked, "So what does metal bending mean?" I often speak until my vocal cords crack about our wonderful potential and how we can create our personal reality. But nothing can prove this potential like a graphic demonstration of an ability the earth's mass consciousness says cannot be done. Bending a spoon is an exercise in transcending this reality.

The key is simple: Thoughts are things. You are what you believe. Change your thoughts—your beliefs—and you can change your life.

—— POSITIVE ACTION STEPS ——

☞ Avoid negative influences and people.

☞ Concentrate on your goals with white-hot intensity.

☞ Keep positive. You can achieve
anything you believe you can.

DAY 40

CREATIVE VISION

Napoleon Hill said: "In every normal mind, a sleeping genius lies waiting for the gentle touch of strong desire to arouse it. The distance from where you are now to the place where you wish to be is but a short distance—regardless of your previous experiences—when you awaken the genius within you."

The human mind is so powerful that it can produce the wealth you desire, the position you long for, the friendship you need, and the qualities that are necessary for the achievement of any worthwhile undertaking.

"Strong desire is the mysterious force which arouses that sleeping genius in the human brain and puts it to work in earnest," Hill said. "Desire is the spark which bursts forth into a flame in the boiler of human effort and generates the steam with which to produce action."

There are many and varied influences that arouse desire and put it to work. Disappointment, sorrow, and adversities of every nature serve to arouse the human mind and cause it to function through new channels.

When you come to understand that failure is only a temporary condition that arouses you to greater action, you will see as plainly as you can see the sky on a clear day that failure is a blessing in disguise. When you come to look upon adversity and failure in this light, you will begin to understand the greatest power on the face of this earth. You will then begin to make capital out of failure instead of allowing it to drag you down.

Hill wrote, "There is a happy day coming in your life when you discover that whatever you aspire to accomplish depends not upon others, but upon you. The arrival of this new day will be preceded by your discovery of the strength of desire!"

Start right now, today, to create a strong and irrepressible desire for the station in life that you wish to attain. Make it the focus of most of your thoughts. Dwell upon it by day and dream about it at night. Keep your mind focused on it during every spare moment. Write it out on paper, and place it where you can see it at all times. Concentrate your every effort toward its realization, and it will materialize itself for you.

Sure, you will make mistakes along the way, but don't let that stop you.

W. Clement Stone, who built a large multinational company with $100 and a positive mental attitude, prided himself on always making the right decision. Of course, he and his employees made as many mistakes as everyone else, but when they made a wrong decision, they went to work to make their wrong decisions right.

He and his associates made it a policy that when someone made a mistake or had a problem, they would use an affirmation such as: "That's good; that's great!" Then they tried to find what was good about it.

They proved again and again that with every adversity, there is the seed of an equivalent or greater benefit. Over the years he made millions for his shareholders because they made the wrong decisions *right*.

When Stone and Napoleon Hill became associated in business, they agreed that such self-motivators were important ingredients of a positive mental attitude. Stone believes that self-motivators are a powerful tool because they capsulize magnificent thoughts—complex concepts—in just a few words that anyone could read and understand. Stone and Hill also believed that the greatest power we human beings have is the power to choose.

One fundamental rule is this: you and I have inherited instincts, emotions, passions, feelings, and tendencies. We develop moods, habits, and impulses. Even the most logical of us don't act from reason alone. We act on emotions and feelings as well as logic. If you understand motivation and how it works in yourself, you also go a long way toward understanding others.

When you can determine what motivates someone else, you will be a better manager because you can inspire your employees to set—and reach—higher and higher goals. You will also become a better parent because you will be better equipped to help your children reach their potential; and—if you understand what motivates someone—you can sell him or her your ideas, your products, or your services.

You can do these things, because you have the power to choose—to make your own decisions and follow through on them. And if you make a wrong decision—make it right.

—— POSITIVE ACTION STEPS ——

☞ You can make a wrong decision right by finding
the seed of opportunity in its adversity.

☞ Use affirmations like "That's good;
that's great!" to keep a positive mental
attitude when faced with setbacks.

☞ Understand how to motivate yourself, and you can
use the same techniques to motivate others.

DAY 41

SPIRITUAL OUTLOOK

I f you have ever pondered questions about spirituality or wondered about life after death, you are not alone. It is a subject that has inspired poets, preachers, and scientists alike.

Dr. Werner von Braun, a NASA scientist who died in 1977, was one of the world's leading authorities on rocketry and a driving force in manned space flight. It was his engineering team that built the rocket that launched America's first satellite and the Saturn V rocket, which put a man on the moon.

You probably know about his achievements in space. But you may not be so familiar with his views on the meaning of life and the hereafter.

Twenty-five years ago in an editorial in *Success* magazine, Dr. von Braun explained how he reconciled his religious faith with science. He said: "In our modern world, many people seem to feel that science has somehow made such 'religious ideas' as immortality untimely or old-fashioned. But I think science has a real surprise for the skeptics."

He said, "Science has found that nothing can disappear without a trace. Nature does not know extinction. All it knows is transformation!"

"Now, if God applies this fundamental principle to the most minute and insignificant parts of His universe," Dr. von Braun said, "doesn't it make sense to assume that He applies it also to the masterpiece of His creation—the human soul? I think it does. And everything science has taught me—and continues to teach me—strengthens my belief in the continuity of our spiritual existence after death. Nothing disappears without a trace."

The great scientist went on to say that after much study, he had concluded that religion and science are indeed compatible, a conclusion that is finding increasing acceptance in today's world.

Dr. von Braun may have been far ahead of his time in calling for a strengthening of the moral and ethical climate in the world to ensure that we wisely use the awesome power we possess in the age of space travel and nuclear power.

Whatever God you worship, or if you have none at all, I think it's worth noting that this great scientist, after considerable reflection and study, concluded that the subject of spirituality merits our attention. It is a very important component of the human existence.

Cynthia Kreuger, author of *Hit the Ground Running: Communicate Your Way to Business Success*, knows about the concept of spiritualism and applied faith. She had a burning desire to succeed in her own business and studied the principles of success. But she says she missed an important point.

"I didn't seek wisdom to know what to do next," she said. "Instead, I chose a business that I thought would fit into my budget."

Even though she didn't particularly like her service business, Kreuger believed that her burning desire and definiteness of purpose could force her success. She explored avenues to introduce her business to the world.

A local newspaper agreed to print her informative columns, she wrote and presented a regular adult education workshop, and she created a newsletter of helpful thoughts that she mailed to would-be clients. She enjoyed these activities, but still her business went nowhere.

She re-examined the principles of success and realized that she had failed to grasp one significant point: applied faith. Further investigation taught her that when you apply faith, you receive the guidance of Infinite Intelligence. She found that faith allows you to tune in to the source of unlimited power and wisdom to attain a definite life's purpose.

Actually, she says she discovered that the guidance was there all along. The business she didn't like was failing while the writing she loved was being accepted in various ways. She said, "I needed to change my focus and grasp the wisdom the universe was offering."

Soon afterward, a publisher's advertisement in a professional association newsletter seemed to jump off the page at her. She called the publisher immediately and within weeks had a contract to turn her workshop into a book. A second book followed, the result of a business communication workshop she developed while promoting the first book.

We must take positive steps to make events work out with full faith that they will lead to good, says Kreuger. She found that it's faith that directs us to open doors. The wisdom of Infinite Intelligence provides the path if we are determined to succeed and have faith that it will lead to our eventual good.

— POSITIVE ACTION STEPS —

☞ Trust that there are forces in the universe
we don't understand, but that if we work
for good, we will attract good things.

☞ Have faith in yourself and your abilities.

☞ Have faith that if you keep trying things
will eventually work out for the best.

DAY 42

MEDITATION

If you sometimes have trouble dealing with stress, you are certainly not alone. When you stop to realize that most stress is self-induced, however, you may discover that it isn't stress that is killing you. It's you that's killing you.

The best way to deal with stressful situations is by not internalizing the problem. Easy to say, but very difficult to do. Here are a few techniques that you may find helpful.

None of us likes to fire people, for example, but if you have to lay off some people at work, there are ways to deal with the stress. If you treat the people involved with as much generosity and compassion as possible, you don't have to agonize over the decision after it's done. You know that you've done the best you could for them. In his book *Welcome Stress! It Can Help You Be Your Best*, Dr. William Brown says another way to deal with stress is to refuse to play the "if only" game.

Saying "if only" allows us to focus on what might have been instead of what is or what can be. If only we had invested in IBM in the late 1950s, if only we had bought a house years ago when prices were lower, or if only we had seized some other lost opportunity.

Dr. Brown recommends substituting "and yet" for "if only." When you do, you vastly improve the odds of success because the emphasis is placed on what you can do about it now instead of worrying about how you missed the boat in the past. It is not too late to turn your life around regardless of how many opportunities you may have missed, how old you are, or where you are now. It starts with forgetting about the past.

Don't waste time trying to figure out how you got where you are today. Instead, spend your time and effort figuring out how you are going to get where you want to be. Take stock of your situation, review your options realistically, then choose the best option given the realities of your situation.

Worrying about things you can't control is not only counterproductive, it's harmful. Studies have shown that needless worry can cloud not just our mental well-being, but our physical condition as well.

One way to minimize stress is to find a hobby. By focusing your mind on something other than the problems of the day, you can immediately lower your anxiety level and, in many cases, even your blood pressure.

Another way to unload stress is to exercise regularly. A half hour a day spent on cardiovascular exercise like vigorous walking or jogging not only gets you in better shape, it also releases endorphins in the brain, which help our bodies relax and deal with stress.

Many have found relief in meditation. For some, meditation is simply a way to relax the body. Others say that meditation can put us in tune with our bodies and allows our minds to communicate thoughts and insights more easily. Tibetan monks have been said to reach such a state of communion with their bodies that they can control involuntary bodily functions like heartbeat and body temperature.

Meditation may also enhance the body's healing processes. Scientific studies have shown that during meditation the amount of oxygen taken in by the body decreases, blood pressure decreases, and alpha waves (brain waves associated with relaxation) become more intense.

To try meditation for yourself, sit quietly in a comfortable position. Close your eyes and silently repeat a pleasant sounding word or phrase over and over. This phrase used to be called a mantra and was typically a phrase from Hindu scripture, but any positive affirmation like "Yes I can" will work.

Many claim that in this relaxed state, their thoughts become clearer and that they sometimes even come up with solutions to problems they have been facing.

Try this technique for fifteen to twenty minutes each morning and each evening before meals. After doing it consistently for a week or so, you may find that meditation is not just a great way to relax, but that it is also a simple way to "center" yourself and get in a positive frame of mind—the proper frame of mind from which all success originates.

—— POSITIVE ACTION STEPS ——

☞ Exercise daily. A half hour of vigorous walking each day can relieve stress and keep you in shape.

☞ Try using positive affirmations like "I can do it" repeated over and over to relax you into a meditative state.

☞ Never spend time worrying over thoughts that begin "If only...."

CHAPTER SEVEN

MAKE IT HAPPEN

The only person responsible for your success is you. This chapter includes articles on sticking to your goals, taking responsibility for your actions, and making success happen.

DAY 43

DEFINITENESS OF PURPOSE

Napoleon Hill said that definiteness of purpose is the starting point of all achievement. You must first know where you are going if you ever have any hope of arriving there.

Definiteness of purpose means you have specific measurable goals for your life and your career, but it is much more. Definiteness of purpose might be described as a road map to your overall career objective while goals represent important milestones along the way. Unless you are one of those extremely rare individuals who has such great talent or mental capacity that you skyrocket to the top, you are an ordinary mortal like most of the rest of us, and you must deliberately, methodically work your way toward your goal. Most architects, for example, wouldn't begin their careers designing multimillion-dollar skyscrapers. They begin with smaller structures or portions of larger buildings until their clients are confident enough in them to risk substantial amounts of capital on their ideas.

Many so called "overnight successes" have spent years preparing themselves for the opportunity that finally affords them the recognition that they deserve.

Having a definite aim for your life has a synergistic effect on your ability to achieve your goals. By specializing, you become better at what you do, you devote more of your time and your resources toward reaching your objective, and you become more alert to opportunities. Everything you see and do will remind you of something related to your goal and you will have more energy and enthusiasm than you've ever had in your life. You will also find that you can reach decisions more quickly. Every action you take will ultimately boil down to the question: "Will this help me reach my overall objective or won't it?"

Most important, having a definite purpose manifests itself in a burning desire that will help you focus all your energies on reaching your goals. When you stumble and fall, you'll pick yourself up and dust yourself off and get right back in the game. When you have the kind of burning desire I'm talking about—the fire in your guts that sustains you no matter how tough things are—nothing can stop you from achieving your goals. You won't even think of giving up until you prevail in your plan. Your purpose will become your life; it will permeate your conscious mind and it will so absorb your subconscious mind that even when you're asleep, you'll be working toward the achievement of your major purpose in life.

Start by asking yourself: Where do I want to be six months from today? Where do I want to be a year from today? Where do I wish to be ten or twenty years from today? If your goals are unclear, sit down with a pencil and paper—right now—and ask yourself: If I had a magic wand, what would I wish for? If I could do anything with my life that I wanted to do, what would it be? You can do anything you wish—if you have the desire to do what is necessary to achieve your goals as long as it doesn't violate the laws of God or the rights of your fellow man.

Write down your goal and take time each day to read it as you've written it down. Carry your written goal with you everywhere you go. Don't let go of that paper until you have reached your goal. Once you have reached it, and you will if you concentrate on it hard enough, replace it with your next goal. Then keep going until all your dreams are realized.

Remember: What the mind can conceive and believe, the mind can achieve with definiteness of purpose and a positive mental attitude. To maintain a positive mental attitude, set aside time each day to think, plan, and dream of ways to reach your goal.

Also it is important to keep motivated. Set aside time each day to study and read motivational materials. As Napoleon Hill observed, "Motivation is like a fire. Unless you add fuel, it soon goes out."

—— **POSITIVE ACTION STEPS** ——

☞ Develop a definite purpose—a goal you
fix in your mind until it is reached.

☞ Keep motivated by reading positive
motivational materials.

☞ Realize that any goal is attainable with
hard work and persistence.

DAY 44

GOING THE EXTRA MILE

There are two types of people in the world, those who say, "When they pay me what I'm worth, then and only then will they get what they pay for."

The other type is just the opposite. They say, "I'm going to give a hundred and ten percent to my job. I'm going to do my best every day of the year—for me—because that's the kind of person I am. I know that I will eventually be recognized and rewarded accordingly."

You don't have to be real smart to figure out which of these two personality types is going to do the best in his or her career. One of them will become a positive person, an achiever, someone others admire. The negative personality types, on the other hand, can only expect a life of failure—failure to realize their dreams, failure to achieve financial success, and failure to become the person they might have been. They will wake up one day and realize that life has passed them by, that the train has already left the station and they didn't even hear the boarding call.

As writer Elbert Hubbard said, "Folks who never do more than they are paid for will never be paid for more than they do."

Napoleon Hill called it "going the extra mile." He maintained that if you render more and better service than that for which you are paid, when you always give a little something extra, every seed of useful service that you sow will come back to you in abundance. Soon or later, you will receive compensation that will far exceed the actual value of the service that you render.

But the money isn't even the best part. Hill also pointed out that when you go the extra mile you build that most important of all success traits—character. When you are known as a person of character, one who always does more than you are expected to do, you will soon find that there is a permanent demand for your services. And just as important, you will soon begin to feel the thrill of new and stronger convictions of courage and self-reliance, new surges of the self-starting power of personal initiative, and an energizing influx of vital enthusiasm.

You, too, can be one of those people who is paid for more than you do. It is absolutely possible, and it's entirely within your control. What's even better, you may soon discover that you actually like going the extra mile. It's all a matter of attitude.

The good character you develop may be even more important when you achieve great success, when you can afford anything you want.

When you have reached high levels of achievement, when others defer to you because of who you are, or when you can have anything you want, you need character and discipline to keep your balance, to maintain your perspective.

How often we hear about sports figures, entertainers, and other celebrities who acquired riches before they had sufficient maturity and character to properly discipline themselves—with disastrous results. Instead of directing their energies in positive pursuits, they squandered their potential on drugs, gambling, or other forms of destructive behavior.

You also need character to sustain you when others try to deter you from your goals. There will always be those who are easily distracted—and seek others to join them—because they have no goals or can never seem to attain them.

Your mother was right about such people. You will never bring them up to your level; they will only drag you down to theirs. Make sure your friends and associates are positive people of good character, individuals who share your values and your desire to do something constructive with your life.

Character building is an ongoing process. It is never finished. I like to think of it as a personal continuous improvement program similar to those advocated by quality management experts.

In fact, all of nature is engaged in a continuous improvement process. Every organism strives continually to improve itself, to grow stronger in order to survive. Animals that can't outrun or outwit predators and plants that cannot adapt to the changing environment will soon be extinct. It is a fact of life.

The same is true with people. Unless we continually improve our capabilities, we will soon become extinct in a society where change—on a scale unprecedented in history—occurs with lightning speed. In this environment it is easy to lose sight of who you are and what you stand for unless you are totally focused and firmly grounded.

—— POSITIVE ACTION STEPS ——

☞ Always do more than is expected of you.

☞ Remember that character building
is an ongoing process.

☞ Associate only with positive people of good
character who share your values.

DAY 45

NO INITIATIVE

G reat achievement results from giving more than what's expected, not just doing what you're told and no more. Neither will you achieve great heights of success by refusing to do as you're told.

It's hard to say which would be more discouraging: drifting from job to job because you're always the first to be laid off—a result of not doing your job as you were told—or laboring in monotonous obscurity at the same job because you only did what you were told to do and no more. You can get by following either approach, but you will never get ahead.

Personal initiative is more important than ever in today's high-tech workplace. Back in the industrial age, the ability to follow orders was a critical skill. But as technology makes many supervisory functions obsolete, every one of us is expected to do more with less—to determine what needs to be done and to do it.

If you are constantly waiting to be told what to do, you will soon find that you are at best unpromotable and at worst replaceable. The world doesn't have time to wait for you. To get ahead, you should know your company and job so well that you can anticipate what needs to be done—then do it.

First, you need to get the big picture. How does what you work on fit into the organization? Nothing is more frustrating to a manager than someone who creates problems because he doesn't know and doesn't care what happens to his work once it leaves his area and goes somewhere else in the organization. If you know where you fit in the organization, which link in the chain you are, you can intercept problems instead of passing them along. And that not only makes you a more valuable employee to your supervisor, it also helps give you a feeling of satisfaction—of contributing to the success of the company.

If you have no idea about how what you do affects the rest of the company, you're less likely to care if you do your job well. Such an attitude leads to carelessness, and you will quickly become someone who is easily replaceable.

Another common problem people fall into is the activity trap. If we're constantly busy, we reason, we must be getting a lot done. The obvious flaw in this assumption is that activity doesn't necessarily produce results.

The key to successful time management is to go after your big, high-payoff goals every day and to minimize the time you spend on those trivial details that take up so much time. There will always be big and little things to do in our lives. Unfortunately, many people who are big picture people at heart often end up spending their time on little details. The danger lies in making a career of focusing on trivial things.

Goal setting will help keep you focused. Identify your goals and go after them. Once you have your definite purpose in life identified, it then becomes a matter of deciding whether or not an activity helps you reach your goal. If it does, it's worth spending time on; if not, it's time to reevaluate.

Some experts estimate that for most of us roughly twenty percent of our efforts generate eighty percent of our results. This principle cuts across virtually every activity. For example, twenty percent of the home usually accumulates eighty percent of the dirt. Clean the high-traffic areas frequently and let the rest wait longer.

The same holds true in sales. Eighty percent of your sales usually come from twenty percent of your customers. Spend more of your time on the customers who give you the most business.

Twenty percent of your employees are probably doing eighty percent of the work; recognize that and reward them accordingly. Not only does this motivate the twenty percent to even higher levels of achievement, but it may catch on with the majority that this is the road to success.

Spend your time in areas that offer the biggest payoff. Do it consistently and your life will end up the biggest payoff of all—your success.

—— POSITIVE ACTION STEPS ——

☞ Always try to do more than you are asked to do.

☞ Determine what really needs to be done—then do it.

☞ Learn more about what other people in your organization do. It will help you figure out where you fit in and how you can contribute more to the company's overall success.

DAY 46

BE YOUR BEST

By his own account, Bud Hadfield was a bad kid. He was expelled from high school twice, and as he said, "I had to get my head pounded a few times to straighten me out."

As a teenager, Hadfield was constantly in trouble. His quick temper led him into fights, and he rebelled against everything. He developed some much-needed personal discipline in the merchant marines during World War II and saved enough money to launch his first business, but still nothing worked out right for him.

He failed in the egg business, as the owner of a pig farm, a gas station operator, the owner of a fireworks stand and a personnel agency. Then he tried the franchise business in picture framing and photo finishing.

"When people tell me there's money in picture framing," he says, "I tell them: 'I know. $300,000 of it is mine!'"

He also had a tough time when he got in the printing business back in the 1960s. Plastic printing plates were new and instant printing centers were springing up all over the country; Hadfield opened one in Houston that he called Kwik Kopy.

In his early days in business, his temper still caused him problems. "It wasn't uncommon for me to have confrontations with customers," he said, "and some of them led to fistfights. It was probably the most unproductive time of my life."

Then two things happened that turned his life around. He started reading motivational self-help books. "I finally realized that I don't have to be the person I am now," he said. "I can be a better person." He also learned about the importance of having a burning desire to achieve success. He poured his energy into Kwik Kopy and began building the business.

Today, Kwik Kopy is the country's largest printing franchise with sales of about $350 million a year, and its operations include five printing and publishing businesses as well as the International Center for Entrepreneurial Development. Hadfield is the Chairman and CEO of the company.

In 1993, to honor his contribution to the franchise industry, at its annual convention in San Juan, Puerto Rico, Bud Hadfield was inducted into the International Franchise Association's Hall of Fame. It was a fitting tribute to the bad boy who made good.

Of course, the key to Hadfield's success was deciding that he was going to do what it took to be the best that he could be. You'd be surprised at what obstacles that kind of thinking can help you overcome.

Brian Holloway, for example, transformed himself—through sheer determination—from a shy, timid, overweight child into an NFL All-Pro offensive lineman with the New England Patriots and Los Angeles Raiders.

"As a child, I was not a very good student," Brian Holloway recalls. "Learning did not come easy. The teachers thought I was a great candidate for drugs, crime, and a life of trouble. I later learned that I was dyslexic, hyperactive, and suffered from attention-deficit disorder."

Holloway told me, "Sports was not a field of dreams for me either. I played six years of Little League baseball and struck out every time at bat without taking a swing—I was too afraid to swing and miss."

An unexpected event provided a source of inspiration for Holloway. He wrote a letter to the St. Louis Cardinals' Bob Gibson just after the team lost the 1968 World Series. He felt compelled to tell Gibson that he still believed the powerhouse pitcher was the greatest.

A year later, Holloway received an envelope at his family's home in Hawaii. It had no stamp and no return address. Inside was an autographed picture of Bob Gibson.

Holloway was overcome with emotion and told his mother, "Bob Gibson found me—Brian Holloway! Five thousand miles away, he found me!"

Holloway resolved that he, too, would achieve greatness in life. He bought a secondhand weight bench and a set of mismatched weights at a yard sale and began working out in his garage "gym." He spent evenings and weekends improving his learning skills and overcoming dyslexia. He went from being the player no one wanted, to being recruited by 350 universities with offers of full scholarships at each.

In 1977, the 6-foot 7-inch 250-pound Holloway graduated high school as a member of the National Honor Society. He's convinced that every person has the capacity to tap into super powers of concentration, strength, and endurance. He uses the example of the mother who in an urgent moment defies all logic and lifts a car off her child who is trapped beneath it.

"My accomplishments," Holloway says, "came about because I was able to harness that super state of power to learn and develop skills I did not have. In this super state you have unlimited power, ingenuity, and creativity."

POSITIVE ACTION STEPS

☞ Accept responsibility for your actions.

☞ Don't make excuses for why you can't do something. Find a way to do it.

☞ Look for solutions, not someone to blame.

DAY 47

DEALING WITH
DISCOURAGEMENT

One of my favorite quotes is from movie producer Michael Todd: "Being broke is temporary; being poor is a state of mind." It illustrates that adversity, like success, is what we make of it.

Most of us don't deal well with adversity. If there is a problem, often we can't rest until a solution is found. Fortunately, there is always an answer. And we can find that answer if we stop needlessly worrying, analyze the situation, and focus on solutions.

When faced with adversity, a helpful technique is to focus immediately on the desired end result. It doesn't matter who caused your current problem; it doesn't matter if your problem is the result of bad or unfair treatment by others; it doesn't even matter if you caused the problem in the first place by making some incredibly stupid mistake. All that matters is how to get out of the undesirable situation in which you find yourself and get back on a positive course.

Japanese businesses have utilized this secret of success for years. They correctly point out that one reason they outperform a lot of American companies is that Americans often waste time fixing the blame instead of fixing the problem.

When you stop worrying and decide to solve a problem, you'll find there are any number of solutions. But don't waste time trying to find that non-existent "perfect" solution. The goal is to find the solution that is the most appropriate under the present circumstances.

After you've decided on the best course of action, focus on implementing it. Don't worry about obstacles that get in the way of executing your plan. If you focus on the problems, you will find problems. If you focus on solutions, you will find solutions. That's why novice hang-glider pilots can hit the only tree in an otherwise open field—because they concentrated on the tree rather than the open spaces.

It is also helpful in those first few panicky moments, when everything seems to have fallen apart, to stop and ask yourself: "What's the worst thing that could happen?" Usually you will find you can live with the answer, and the problem will shrink to its appropriate level of importance.

Soon you will become more confident in your decisions. And as we often see, people with self-confidence seem to somehow rise above the rest. Success seems to come to them easily and naturally.

If you dig a little deeper, however, you will very likely find that their confidence is the result of a long painstaking process any one of us can use. It may be easier for some than for others, but the principles can be easily learned and can be applied by anyone.

Here are some techniques that you can use to become a positive thinker, a confident person who sees success possibilities instead of the potential for failure.

First, begin each day positively. Think about the things you are grateful for, the things that make you happy, not the problems and all the things you wish you could accomplish but probably never will.

Second, whenever possible, avoid stressful situations. If petty arguments upset your day before you leave home, try leaving before other family members begin the usual morning rush. Go to work early occasionally, catch up on chores you've been avoiding, or read the newspaper with your morning coffee.

Third, associate with positive people. Your mother was right when she told you that your worthless friends will only drag you down. Plus, it's a lot harder to be positive when you waste your time with negative thinkers.

Fourth, learn from experience. If you have a tendency to be negative, review your behavior each day while it is still fresh in your memory. Analyze your actions and determine what you should do differently to be more positive.

Fifth, be realistic. Set achievable goals for yourself and break them into bite-sized pieces. Try to do at least one thing every day that moves you toward your goal.

Sixth, take calculated risks. If you never take a chance, you will never achieve anything worthwhile. Risk rejection of your idea as long as you're convinced it is sound.

Finally, do something nice for someone without expecting anything in return. It keeps them off balance and it makes you feel great about yourself.

POSITIVE ACTION STEPS

☞ Fix the problems, not the blame.

☞ Don't let setbacks stop you. Visualize your goal and work harder to achieve it.

☞ Anticipate problems, and be ready to work through them.

DAY 48

THE OPTIMISTIC ENTREPRENEUR

It's no accident that the guy who invented the zipper didn't come from the button industry, and the inventor who patented Velcro wasn't a zipper manufacturer. Experts tend to focus on what won't work instead of concentrating on new possibilities.

Professor Gary Hamel, a professor at the London Business School, says the seeds of foresight lie in those who have a pervasive sense of restlessness with the status quo. Innovators are always looking for new ideas and better ways. They have a deep and boundless curiosity. They like to explore new ideas simply because it's fun. They also have a childlike innocence. They are not constrained by conventional wisdom that says something must be done a certain way simply because that's the way it's always been done.

Innovators also look outside their industries for new ideas. Dr. Hamel points to the airline industry as a perfect example of myopic thinking. For years, it has been an accepted fact in the industry that the only way to operate an airline is on the hub and spokes system. Airplanes fly out of hubs and up and down spokes to the various destinations they serve.

Then along came Virgin Atlantic and Southwest Airlines. They don't use the hub and spokes system. And they do radical things to differentiate themselves.

Southwest bills itself as a "fun" airline. Its people wear shorts and tell jokes over the intercom.

Virgin Airlines thinks more like a cruise line than an airline. Virgin believes that the trip should be as much fun as arriving at the destination. So it offers blackjack, private VCRs, and a selection of videos on board.

Maybe that's why most of the major players in the industry seem to be constantly going into or emerging from bankruptcy while Virgin Atlantic and Southwest are two of only a handful of profitable airlines. They can foresee the future because they are helping to invent it.

The entrepreneurs who started these companies also had the foresight to surround themselves with the right teams of people.

This isn't always the case. Many successful entrepreneurs are convinced that because they are good at some things, they can do anything. Because they invented a product, for example, they think they can also sell it. Or because they're great at sales, they can also run the company. They believe that the power of their enthusiasm and conviction will see them through.

Being a successful entrepreneur does require an abundance of optimism and a healthy measure of self-confidence, but as in many aspects of life, our greatest strengths are also our greatest weaknesses. Enthusiasm needs to be counter balanced by self-discipline and accurate thinking. If you're good at selling and working with others, but not so proficient at running the office, perhaps your answer lies in aligning yourself with others whose strengths complement your weaknesses. If you are a good salesperson, for example, make sure you have a good business management person on your team. Find someone who has the patience to set up and run the systems needed for day to day management of a business.

If you are the entrepreneurial type, objectively determine what you like to do and are good at, and the things you hate and are not so good at. Then find others who have the skills and interests that you lack.

It may not be easy to find perfect partners, but it's worth the effort. Two or more people who work well together toward a common objective can accomplish far more than any of them could accomplish by working separately.

At first, it may be hard giving up some of the control you once had, but you'll eventually realize that doing so simply frees you to do those things you like doing best. And soon, you'll find that both of you are accomplishing awe-inspiring results.

—— POSITIVE ACTION STEPS ——

☞ Allow your curiosity to help you find
better ways to do things.

☞ Don't allow yourself to be constrained
by conventional wisdom.

☞ Realize your shortcomings and find partners
who can complement your talents.

DAY 49

YOU ARE THE MASTER OF YOUR FATE

In William Henley's famous poem "Invictus," we find these powerful lines: "It matters not how strait the gate, how charged with punishments the scroll, I am the master of my fate: I am the captain of my soul."

There is no doubt that if you ever hope to achieve success in life, you must become the master of your own fate. And there is a price to be paid. Part of the price, according to W. Clement Stone, is to engage in study, thinking, and planning. He suggests we study, think, and plan daily the goals we wish to set for ourselves and our families, regarding our development or the acquisition of anything in life that we desire—regardless of how ambitious those objectives may be.

Stone says that you, like every other living person, posses a machine so awesome that only God himself could create it: a brain and a nervous system—a human computer. But for your human computer to function properly, you must learn how to use it.

"Our school systems haven't taught us how to direct our thoughts, control our emotions, and ordain our destinies by scientifically releasing and controlling the power of our subconsciousness," he says, "but these things can be learned by you or anyone else willing to take the time to study and understand the workings of the human mind. You must learn about your instincts, tendencies, passions, emotions, moods, feelings, habits of thought, and actions, and how to use them to set and achieve them."

Stone suggests that you begin by resolving to change your life for the better by putting in action the principles you find in motivational literature and self-help books. You become the master of your own fate and captain of your soul by first deciding that you and you alone determine what you will do with your life. Recognize that there are events you cannot control, but that you can always control your attitude toward those events. You can take charge of your life and assume responsibility for your own success.

We all face adversity at times, but how you react to it will determine whether or not you are the best, according to actor, broadcaster, businessman, and popular professional speaker Bill Clement.

Clement is a good example of someone who has taken responsibility for his success. "I've been at the bottom and on top, and I passed through the middle on my way up and my way down. I can tell you there's only one thing worth aspiring to be, and that is to be the best," Clement said.

As far back as he can remember, Clement was a super-achiever. He played minor league hockey at age fifteen and turned pro at nineteen. By the time he was twenty-five, he had won two Stanley Cup Championships with the Philadelphia Flyers.

When he retired from professional hockey, Clement entered the restaurant business with the same intensity that he played hockey, but he quickly learned that intensity wasn't enough in the highly competitive and fickle restaurant business. Within two years he was bankrupt. Not only had he failed personally, he had lost a lot of other people's money as well. Plus, he had no job, no training, no college education, no career, and no money. Clement turned to acting as a new career and applied the principles of success he read about in self-help books. He honed his skills, got a few breaks, and decided to make the commitment. He would move to New York to pursue his dream.

He arrived with no job, no prospects, no agent, and just enough money to cover expenses for three months. But he had a plan and a burning desire to succeed.

He attacked acting with a vengeance, landing roles in more than 250 commercials. He became ESPN's top hockey analyst and rejoined the Flyers as the team's TV analyst. He has covered the Stanley Cup playoffs, the NHL All-Star games, and the Winter Olympics. In 1993, Clement won Cable TV's top award as the best analyst in any sport.

Recalling the obstacles he had to overcome, Clement said, "I now know that the world doesn't care how many times you get knocked down, only how many times you get back up."

—— POSITIVE ACTION STEPS ——

☞ Resolve that you will take responsibility
for your own future.

☞ Read, study, and put into practice the
proven principles of success.

☞ Identify the principles in this book that you plan to
put into practice, then get into action to apply them.

CHAPTER EIGHT

DO UNTO OTHERS

Successful people know how to treat others. Week Eight includes articles about how to get along with others, both personally and professionally.

_____

DAY 50

SERVING OTHERS
WILL HELP YOU

John Wanamaker, the Philadelphia merchant king, once said that the most profitable habit is that of "rendering useful service where it is not expected."

Napoleon Hill added that one of the surest ways to achieve your own success is by helping others to attain theirs. But Hill also cautioned that it takes a conscious effort to give your time and energy to others. You can't simply say, "All right, I'm willing to help anyone who needs my help."

He suggested making a creative project out of rendering service to your fellow man. Hill offered a few down-to-earth examples to help you think of ways you can win friends by helping others.

A few years ago, there was a merchant out East who built a successful business through a very simple process. Every hour or so, one of his clerks checked the parking meters near the store. When the clerk spotted an expired meter, he dropped a coin in the slot and attached a note to the car. It said that the merchant was pleased to protect him against the inconvenience of a parking ticket. Many motorists dropped in to thank the merchant—and remained to buy something.

Another example was of the owner of a big Boston men's store who inserted neatly printed cards in the pocket of each suit he sold. It told the purchaser that if he found the suit satisfactory, he could take the card back after six months and exchange it for any necktie he chose. Naturally, the buyer always came back pleased with the suit and was a ripe prospect for another sale.

And finally, the highest paid woman employee of the Banker's Trust Co. in New York City got her start by offering to work for three months without pay in order to demonstrate her executive ability, at no risk to the bank.

Actually, there's a very good and selfish reason to lend a hand to others in need. Regardless of how capable or how independent you may be, there will come a time when you will have to call on someone else for help.

When I was a kid growing up on a farm in Oklahoma, I learned a lesson about the practical aspects of helping others that has lasted a lifetime. My dad had assigned me to drive the tractor from our home to a field a few miles away with instructions to take the back roads to avoid traffic, to drive especially slowly because a recent rain had made the roads muddy and slippery, and not to stop for anything. I liked driving the tractor, and I cheerfully set off on my mission. But I was a little selective in following the instructions.

I was having great fun slipping and sliding on the muddy roads when I came upon a couple of farmers who had slid off the road and stuck their pickup truck in the ditch. They yelled for me to stop and give them a hand, but remembering my Dad's order not to stop for anything, I ignored them. I had driven less than a mile when the same fate befell me.

Driving too fast, I suddenly slipped off the road. The more I tried to escape, the deeper I slid into the ditch. I was hopelessly stuck when the two men I had passed earlier came driving slowly in my direction. I was too embarrassed to ask them for help, but they stopped anyway.

With very little conversation, they slogged around in the mud, attached a chain to my tractor, and pulled me out of the ditch. When I asked how I might repay them, one of the men, a kindly old fellow, said: "It's not necessary to pay us. We're happy to be able to help you. But the next time you see someone in trouble, don't drive on by like you don't see them. Stop and lend a hand. And when you do, think about this experience. That will be payment enough for us."

I can tell you that single experience made an indelible impression upon me. I realized that there are times when you can't simply follow instructions. You must use your own good sense. I never forgot that old fellow's kindness, and I've spent a lifetime paying him back.

I think that's what Napoleon Hill meant when he said that when you treat others as you would like to be treated, you set in motion a force for good that will return to you many times over.

—— POSITIVE ACTION STEPS ——

☞ Deal with others as if your reputation
were on the line—it is.

☞ Treat everyone as you would want to be treated.

☞ Don't settle for what's expected of
you. Go the "extra mile."

DAY 51

KEEPING YOUR MOUTH SHUT

We often think that the people who achieve the greatest success in business are the smooth talkers who can charm others into doing what they ask. There are times, though, when silence is definitely golden.

Effective leaders know there are times to speak and times to listen, and they also know that it's never a good idea to gossip about others. When you talk about others behind their backs, it is inevitable that what you say will get back to them. Then you will find yourself in the unhappy position of having to defend yourself and trying to explain why you said what you did. And there's a good chance that by the time your words have traveled that distance, whatever you said will be distorted and even more offensive. Also, you can be sure that something that was said about someone who wasn't around will not be nearly as funny or clever in their presence as it was when you were joking about them with others.

In any business or organization, there always seem to be little cliques of people whose primary recreation is gossiping about others. They never seem to figure out that their behavior not only disrupts the company and unjustly damages the reputations of others, it also reflects badly on them. These people should be avoided at all costs. Just associating with them may give other more responsible people the impression that you are like the people with whom you socialize.

Besides, people who make it a practice to talk about others often forget who said what about whom. You may find that things have been attributed to you that you never said. It's also true that people who gossip are almost never promoted into responsible jobs—and if they are, they don't last in them—because they can't be trusted.

If you can't keep your mouth shut about people in the organization, it's highly unlikely that management is going to entrust you with confidential information about new products, proposed mergers or acquisitions, or any other sensitive issues. If you do show others that they can ask your advice about any subject without worrying whether you are going to disclose it, your counsel will soon be widely sought by your co-workers and others in the company. You will gain their respect because they know they can trust you. And when you have the trust and respect of those with whom you work, you have taken a big step toward becoming a leader.

The thing to keep in mind is when you do something—anything—you set in motion a force that will return to you multiplied many times. What you do or say about others will come back to you and either help you or haunt you.

Some years ago, I got into a dispute with a car rental agent over a misunderstanding that could have and should have been easily and quickly resolved. When I attempted to return the car at the Detroit airport near where I lived, the Detroit agent phoned the agent in London, Ontario, where I had rented the car.

It turned out that in the usual rush that goes on at airports, when I told the agent that I would like to drop the car in Detroit, she misunderstood and thought I was driving to Toronto. When I checked in at the Detroit airport rental car counter, the London agent insisted upon speaking to me. When she learned that her car had been driven out of the country, she was incensed.

"Why did you drive our car to the United States?" she demanded.

"I told you I was going to Detroit when I rented it," I told her.

"You did not," she said. "You said you were going to Toronto. You cannot take our car out of the country."

To which I replied, "Well, it's here. You figure out how to get it back."

Moments before, I had told the Detroit rental agent that I would be going back to Canada within a few days and that if they had not returned the car by then, I would rent it again and drive it back. But after my conversation with the London rental agent, I wasn't about to do anything for that company.

Further, what the agent didn't know was that her company had submitted a proposal to become the primary rental car firm for the company for which I worked. It was a contract that would mean millions of dollars in annual revenues. My rental experience with the company wasn't the only factor in the decision, of course, but it did demonstrate rather vividly that the customer service the company promised didn't match the reality.

We went with another company, and the counter agent who had a hand in losing the business never knew that she had set in motion a negative force that returned to cost her company millions. How different things might have been if only she had been pleasant, cooperative, and helpful.

Think how different things would be for us if we greeted every situation with a positive, cooperative attitude. The old saying,

"What goes around eventually comes around," is true. Make sure what you send around is positive.

—— POSITIVE ACTION STEPS ——

☛ Never engage in gossip.

☛ Never associate with those who engage in gossip.

☛ Always treat others as you would like to be treated.

DAY 52

COS COB: GOING THE EXTRA MILE

How can a small business possibly compete these days against the mega-corporations with millions to spend on advertising? By using a form of advertising most big companies seem to have forgotten about: word of mouth.

Steve Mecsery is the proprietor of Cos Cob TV, a curious blend of television sales, service, and video rentals. His store is in an affluent section of Greenwich, Connecticut, and serves some of the wealthiest people in the nation. But nearby are the low-income housing developments of Stamford, which means Mecsery also serves some of the country's poorest people as well. He treats both groups the same—with warm hospitality, friendly service, and quality products, including rebuilt models that he personally guarantees for 90 days.

Mecsery recalled one customer who lived in one of the low-income housing units in Stamford. The used set she bought failed just two days after the ninety-day warranty had expired. He would have been perfectly justified in sympathizing with the customer and no more; after all, the warranty had run out. But Mecsery doesn't do business that way. He took the set back without question and gave the customer another rebuilt set.

Over the course of the next few days, four new customers from the same housing development came in to buy used sets.

Mecsery's customer had told all her friends about the honest guy at Cos Cob TV who goes the extra mile in serving his customers.

"Word of mouth advertising is far more effective than print ads in my business," Mecsery says. "The way you treat one customer can pass on to any number of his or her friends and neighbors—good or not so good. Just do what you think is right for all your customers, and by that I mean being fair and honest and going that extra step, too. Before you know it, word will get around that your business is a place where people want to come and trade. It really works—and it makes life a lot nicer."

If Steve Mecsery had adopted the attitude of a lot of businesses—that is, cozying up to only the affluent customers—he would have lost the business that came along by going the extra mile for one of his poorest customers.

Going the extra mile for customers is still the most economical and productive form of advertising. Yet very few businesses seem to recognize this fact. You will automatically differentiate yourself from the competition when you do more than what's expected of you.

It's become almost a cliché these days to talk about customer service, yet most business really don't deliver on their big promises of putting the customer first. If they did, they would be creating customers for life.

A recent experience illustrates this. Where we live, there is an unusual delivery service called "Door-to-Door." The company publishes a selection of menus from a number of the best restaurants in the area. Customers can choose from any of them, place the order with the delivery service, which, in turn, places the order with the appropriate restaurant. The Door-to-Door driver then goes to the restaurant, picks up the food, places it in a special insulated container, and delivers it to your door, piping hot and fresh—all for a nominal delivery charge.

It's a family tradition at our home that every Friday evening we order out from Door-to-Door. It's the perfect way to end a long week. Whatever restaurant we choose, the service is almost always flawless, but a few weeks ago there was an exception. The dispatcher phoned us several times to advise us about the status of our order, but when the food finally arrived it was more than an hour late.

When the driver came to the door, he said, "There is no charge for your order. I'm very sorry I'm so late, I just moved here from Iowa and haven't quite learned my way around yet. Next time, I'll do better."

Of course we were pleased to have a free dinner, but by the time we'd finished, Merrilee and I agreed that the company had gone beyond the extra mile. They had done more than was necessary. We phoned the dispatcher and said, "Your driver was very gracious and apologetic, and the food was fine despite the delay. You don't have to give it to us; we want to pay for it."

The dispatcher said "No, that would be unfair to you. How about if we split the difference and you pay half the price?"

I don't know if Door-to-Door has a mission statement, or an employee empowerment program or any of the other buzzwords that are popular in business today. I only know that its employees took the initiative to do the right thing in every interaction with an unhappy customer. I also know that we will be Door-to-Door customers for life.

— POSITIVE ACTION STEPS —

☞ Treat co-workers and customers as
you would want to be treated.

☞ When you make a mistake, own up to
it and do your best to correct it.

☞ Remember: Helping others helps you.

DAY 53

NOT MY FAULT

Four of the deadliest words in the English language are: "It's not my fault." When you start making excuses for why you can't succeed, you have already failed. It doesn't matter what kind of problems you had as a child, the color of your skin, whether or not your family had money, your ethnic background, or where you went to school. The only thing that really matters is your attitude.

I've spent a lot of years trying to figure out what makes people successful so I could tell my readers the secrets of their success. I can tell you one thing for certain. There are a whole lot of successful people who started with nothing, and there are a lot of failures who seemed to have every advantage when they were growing up. They had every advantage, that is, except one: Whatever went wrong was never their fault. They never accepted responsibility for their actions. When things went wrong, someone else was always to blame.

Successful people don't think that way. They take responsibility for themselves and for their people. When something goes wrong—and things always seem to have a way of going wrong— they look for a solution, not for somebody to blame.

They don't make excuses either. Instead of rationalizing why they can't do something, they search for ways to overcome obstacles. They know that just as defeat is never permanent, neither is success. It is something that is earned every day.

You reach the top of your business or profession one step at a time. Big successes come from doing a lot of little things right, often for a lot longer than you expected.

Successful people don't expect to go from the bottom to the top in one giant leap. They know that if they do the right things and do them well, they will eventually prevail. They don't expect someone else to do it for them, and they don't blame their failures on a subordinate or on circumstances beyond their control.

You may find many different personality types at the top of your company, your business, or your profession, but one type you won't find is an excuse maker. They never get that far.

Successful people accept failure for what it is—a learning process. Napoleon Hill said failure is nature's plan for training a person for worthwhile work in life. It is Nature's great crucible and tempering process that burns the dross from all the other human qualities and purifies the metal so it will withstand all hard usage through life. Failure is the great "Law of Resistance" that makes a person stronger in proportion to the extent he overcomes this resistance.

In every failure, there is a great and lasting lesson if one will only think, analyze, and profit from it. Failure develops tolerance, sympathy, and kindness in the human heart. You will not travel very far down life's pathway before you discover that every adversity and every failure is a blessing in disguise—a blessing because it has put your mind and your body in action and thereby causes both to grow through the law of use.

Look back down the ages and you will find history full of incidents that show clearly the cleansing, purifying, strengthening value of failure. When you begin to realize that failure is a necessary part of one's education, you will no longer look upon it with fear. No person ever arose from the knockout blow of defeat without being stronger and wiser in one respect or another.

If you will look back over your own failures you will no doubt see that those failures marked certain turning points in your life and in your plans that were of benefit to you. It is only through our failures that we develop the strength, courage, and wisdom to persevere until we achieve our chief goal in life.

Failure is Nature's greatest gift to those who will only accept it and learn to profit from it.

—— POSITIVE ACTION STEPS ——

☞ Fix the problem instead of trying to fix the blame.

☞ Think of every failure as a learning opportunity.

☞ Failure helps you develop the strength, courage, and wisdom necessary to succeed.

DAY 54

COMPANIONS, ETHICS, AND ANNOYANCES

Your mother was right about choosing your friends carefully. When you spend time with people of courage and integrity, you tend to try to develop the same traits in yourself. Your expectations are automatically raised.

Unfortunately, the reverse is true. Research has shown that it is virtually impossible for a group to transcend itself and become better than the lowest common denominator of the group. Individuals may break out occasionally, but the entire group seldom rises to reach its full potential. As your mother said, you will never bring others up to your level; they will only drag you down to theirs.

It's also important to note that what's legal isn't necessarily what's right. My friend Joan Krga, a senior executive with a Chicago public relations firm, has an interesting observation about ethics and law. Though they are often viewed as identical, they are quite different.

The law is about what can be done without getting in trouble, while ethics is about what you should be doing regardless of the law. That's another way of saying that you need a firm grounding, a code of personal conduct that exceeds the legal minimums. If you have such a standard for yourself, you never need worry about getting in trouble.

Krga also has an interesting way of dealing with life's little annoyances. When dealing with an aggravating situation, she stops and asks herself, "What is really going on here?"

By focusing on specific things that upset her, she can identify problems and solve them.

One of the most positive people I know, she also has a positive approach to getting the most out of life. She makes it a point to find joy in something every day. It doesn't have to be a big success—a cheery greeting from a friend or doing one thing a little better than usual will suffice.

The secret to finding happiness and figuring out what is really right for you is to look inside yourself. Only you have the answers.

Not long ago, I was talking to my friend Walter O'Connor, the dean of the tax department at Fordham University in New York. I met Walter when he was vice chairman of international operations for KPMG Peat Marwick, the big six accounting firm, when I worked there. We laughed as he compared his modest office at the university to his palatial digs at Peat Marwick. He was earning less money and his office was smaller, yet he was happier than he'd ever been.

As we reminisced about our days at the accounting firm, Walter made a very astute observation. What often happens to people, he said, is that we look around us and we compare ourselves to other people we work with and we say, "Look at that guy. I'm better than he is and he's earning $200,000 a year. I ought to be earning $200,000 a year, too." Then we become unhappy because we're not.

What we really should be doing is focusing on our own opportunities and abilities and not worrying about what others around us are doing. You have only one true competitor in life, and that person is yourself.

Years ago in his book *Where Have All the Salesmen Gone?* Wally Armbruster wrote this tribute to the ultimate competitor.

He said, "For me, the ultimate competitor exists within myself. You can only find yours within yourself. The difference between this competitor and the others is that you can never beat him—or her. He is always a shade ahead. As you get stronger, so does he; each time you reach a new level of excellence, he shows you a new level you had never seen before. Each time, he challenges you to give more, try harder, reach higher, dig deeper, do better than you've ever done before. There is no perfect score, not even for him.

"The ultimate competitor is so demanding that he can sometimes be depressing, or at least a (big pain). But he is the only thing that makes the game worthwhile. He is fantastic fun to compete with. But if I ever beat him, I will know that I have lost."

—— POSITIVE ACTION STEPS ——

☞ Spend time with people of courage and integrity—stay away from "bad apples."

☞ Look to yourself, not others, for happiness.

☞ Your ultimate competitor is you.

DAY 55

WORKING WITH PROBLEM BOSSES

Your boss is unreasonable, a workaholic, or a nitpicker. You don't like it, but you still have to deal with him or her. Fortunately there are number of constructive things you can do (short of quitting) to make working with problem bosses a little easier.

People are promoted because they have done well in their jobs. They move up and become the boss. Although they have been great at their original jobs, they may be less effective as the boss.

All bosses can be problem bosses in one way or another. And although yours may have many great qualities, he or she may also have faults that are difficult to tolerate.

Here are some ways to deal with a few of the more difficult types of bosses: If your boss is a shouter, wait until he or she calms down before trying to talk things out. Ignore the anger; there's nothing personal in it. The shouting boss treats everyone that way.

If you have a workaholic boss, get him or her to set priorities and deadlines. This will keep your boss from constantly invading your work and personal time because he or she will know exactly what you're doing and how long it's going to take to do it. Also make it clear that your personal time is important too and isn't to be interrupted by needless calls to check on things.

The "nitpicker" type of boss needs something to constantly worry about. Again, ask this boss to set priorities. He may accept work he would otherwise ask you to endlessly redo when he is made to realize what other tasks could be put on hold because of it. The nitpicker is not good at nurturing—you'll have to find encouragement from someone else in the company.

The "isolated boss." If your boss doesn't communicate and keep you informed, simply determine the best course of action on your own. Tell your boss what you've decided to do unless you hear otherwise. This gives your boss an appropriate amount of control without paralyzing yourself through inaction.

Chances are, no matter how difficult your boss is, you are partly to blame. Without realizing it, you may be encouraging your boss to indulge in his or her objectionable behavior. Talk to other people in the company who know both of you know and get some objective advice.

If you can determine how you are contributing to the problem, you can change your behavior and help create a better boss for yourself.

Of course, there may come a time when you have to deal with a new boss. Your future working relationship may depend more than you think on how you hit it off at the beginning.

Until you have had the opportunity to get to know each other, it's natural for both of you to evaluate each other's working style and compatibility. When you find yourself in this situation, it is not the time to wait and see what happens. You need to get into action, to be proactive, to establish your credentials and your willingness to work with the new boss.

Here are a few things to keep in mind:

☞ Evaluate yourself as though you were meeting you for the first time. Be open to change. People have different styles and your boss may change things—a lot. Be prepared and ready to cooperate.

☞ Don't stay away just to give him or her time to adjust. Introduce yourself right away, discuss projects you're working on, and make sure your work is in line with the boss' objectives.

☞ Determine what your boss' long- and short-term goals are so you can target your work toward achieving them.

☞ Learn all you can about the new department head or supervisor. Talk to people who worked for him or her before. Learn what the boss likes and doesn't like.

☞ Don't waste time telling your new boss about "how we've always done things around here." Find out if he would to try a different approach.

☞ Don't take criticism personally when it comes to you, and don't seek approval when it's not necessary.

☞ Let the boss know your strengths. Give him or her an honest assessment of your abilities. This could be valuable information when different teams are formed or projects assigned.

☞ If you don't seem to be getting along, learn by observing those who do.

☞ Support the new boss and say favorable things about the change to others. If you can't say something positive, don't say anything at all.

Like it or not, the boss is in charge. Most of the responsibility for making the relationship work is yours. But if you train your new boss right, you will have a valuable advisor, friend, and mentor—someone who can be a great asset to your career.

—— POSITIVE ACTION STEPS ——

☞ If you are having problems with your boss, ask him or her what you might do to improve the situation.

☞ Have your boss set priorities. If he won't, set your own priorities, and ask the boss if he would like to change them.

☞ Remember: Whatever you think of the boss, she is still the boss. Most of the responsibility for making it work rests with you.

DAY 56

A POSITIVE APPROACH TO NEGOTIATION

S uccess in negotiation is like success in life. In order to do well, you must first have a goal set firmly in mind. Once you know what you wish to accomplish, there are a few things you can do to get it.

First, you need a positive mental attitude. A positive attitude should be the starting point for almost everything you do in business. If you approach negotiation with a positive attitude, your behavior will tell others that you are confident, self-assured, and trustworthy. They will respond to you accordingly.

Next, you need to recognize that negotiation is a gradual process. Just jumping in will show your counterpart that you are too eager to reach a settlement and will give a lot away to reach one. Start by first getting to know each other. A little socialization can help build trust and help you size up your counterpart. Just be careful not to give away any valuable information while chitchatting.

It also helps to understand others' objectives. What are their needs? What are they hoping to accomplish? Do they need to reach a settlement quickly? Are they representing others who may have set the agenda?

Know your subject inside and out before you get to the table. Evaluate what each item in the negotiation really means to you, which of those items you could give up, and alternate ways to get what you really want. Knowledge is power. Do your research.

Be flexible. A common mistake is to try to force others to your point of view. Remember that your opponent also has certain needs to satisfy. Seek a win-win solution in which both parties walk away happy.

Don't be pressured into a premature agreement. No deal is a good deal if you have not had adequate time to consider it carefully. If you need more time to think about a proposed solution, ask for it. Better yet, sleep on it.

A good night's sleep can help you sort out a complex issue. According to psychotherapist Armand DiMele writing in the *Brain/Mind Bulletin,* his patients observed that, "Sleep is a process of taking whatever information that is gathered during the day and integrating it into the mind of the sleeper...the purpose of sleep is not repair, but integration, learning, growth."

Once you have given your mind a chance to evaluate and integrate the information gained through negotiations, you can better decide if a proposed resolution to the negotiations is one you can live with.

Finally, be sure to listen and observe as much as you talk. Listening is what makes win-win solutions possible. You may have a preconceived notion about a counterpart's motivations, but what they say and especially how they say it may give you clues as to his or her ultimate objective. You always learn more when you listen. Your counterpart may even reveal some critical information if you let him talk long enough.

—— POSITIVE ACTION STEPS ——

☞ In negotiations, strive for "win-win" situations
in which both parties leave happy.

☞ Encourage workers with incentives
tied to performance.

☞ Listen at least as much as you talk.

CHAPTER NINE

WHEN DO WE GET THERE?

Success is a journey. So how do we know when, if ever, we've reached it? This chapter includes a definition of success and gives a few hints for sticking with it until you reach your objective.

DAY 57

WHAT IS SUCCESS?

If your life should tragically end today, how would your obituary read? Would you be remembered as you would like?

I'm sure you've heard of the Nobel Prizes, but there is something about Alfred Nobel, the Swedish chemist and inventor, that you may not know.

As the story goes, several years before Nobel died, as he was reading his morning newspaper, his eye suddenly landed upon his own obituary. What had happened was that his brother had passed away, and the newspaper had accidentally published Alfred Nobel's obituary instead.

Another thing that you may not know about Alfred Nobel is that it was he who in 1863 got a patent on a mixture of nitroglycerin and gunpowder, and three years later refined the process to patent a new product called dynamite.

As he read his own obituary that morning, Alfred Nobel realized that the thing he would most be remembered for was his invention of dynamite—an instrument of destruction. Having been afforded a rare opportunity to see his own future and contemplate his mortality, Nobel vowed to change things. He was determined that he would use his wealth and fame to create a force for good. And that is how the prestigious prizes that bear his name originated.

How would any of us react if we could see our lives through the eyes of an obituary writer? Are you the kind of person you would like to be? Are you living a life that you would be proud for your kids and grandkids to examine and emulate? It's not too late to change. Like Alfred Nobel, you can be remembered as a purveyor of destruction or as one who created a force for good. It's all in how you choose to live your life.

You don't even need millions of dollars to make a difference. Even though we may not all have the financial wherewithal to endow a chair at our favorite university, we can all give something back to the community. In fact, these days the commodity in shortest supply in most groups is time. If you don't have much money to donate, you can still make a major contribution by joining a group whose mission you support. You can volunteer to work on a committee or project that allows you to contribute your expertise to the cause.

Participation in such groups has some very pragmatic benefits, as well. It gives you the opportunity to learn new skills and to make business and professional contacts with community leaders who might otherwise be difficult to meet. Most successful people are involved in civic, charitable, and industry groups.

It is also true that you get out of life what you put into it. If you give generously of your time and money to help those who are less fortunate than you are, you become a better person, one who attracts other good and positive people.

There are very few of us who cannot find a little time to donate to a worthwhile cause. In fact, philanthropic organizations have learned the wisdom in the old saw: "If you want something done, get a busy person to do it." They know that people with time on their hands are those who never get around to doing what needs to be done.

Make sure you're one of the doers, one of the busy people who can always find a little time to help others. When you do, the greatest beneficiary of your generosity will be you.

—— POSITIVE ACTION STEPS ——

☞ Live a life you would be proud to
have others read about.

☞ Determine if your ultimate goal is
worthy of a lifetime of effort.

☞ Realize that it is never too late to
change the direction of your life.

DAY 58

SUCCESS DEFINED

When asked about the secret of his success, millionaire Del Smith said, "Thank God, I was born poor—I learned how to work."

Orphaned as an infant and raised in poverty, today Smith is worth an estimated $600 million and his Evergreen International Aviation empire spans the globe. Not bad for a kid who used to throw cow chips at passing coal trains.

He didn't do it out of spite, but rather to entice the workers into throwing chunks of coal back at him. At the time it was the only way his family could get coal to heat their home.

To help support the family, he managed three paper routes and mowed lawns with a mower he bought for $5.00. By age seven, Smith established credit with local banks and by age ten, he had saved enough for a down payment on a small family cottage in Centralia, Washington.

Hard work coupled with setting specific goals helped Smith accomplish things he'd only dreamed of as a child. He earned his pilot's license by polishing planes to pay for flying lessons. He paid his way through college by working nights and summers at a logging camp. After a stint in the Air Force, he became a helicopter pioneer using helicopters to aid in famine relief, to string power lines, and even to spray fertilizers with a system he himself invented.

In 1960, he founded Evergreen Aviation on the philosophy of "Quality Without Compromise." Smith and his team fervently believe that performance is the only thing that counts; that looking after the customer is the company's only reason for being; and that what the company does should be beneficial for mankind.

Smith's philosophy, backed by a lot of hard work, has paid off. Evergreen has operated in more than 135 countries and flown support missions for such prestigious clients as NASA and the United Nations.

Smith says, "God gave us life; we owe Him our best performance." If his rags to riches story is any indication, the true secret of success is simply: Set your goals, then work as hard as you possibly can to reach them.

Of course, a good deal of persistence doesn't hurt either, as the following story illustrates.

Years ago, the Swiss inventor Georges de Mestral went for a walk in the woods with his dog. When he returned home, he discovered that as he had walked along lost in thought, he had wandered through a patch of cockleburs. Instead of being annoyed, as most of us would have been, he was fascinated by the holding power of the burrs.

He put one under a microscope and found that the cockleburs had hundreds of tiny hooks that had become entangled in the nap of his trousers and in the hair of his dog's coat. *What a great technique*, he thought. *If I could duplicate that process, I could make a lightweight fastener that would work for all sorts of things.*

He began to experiment, and in a relatively short period of time he was able to duplicate the holding properties of the cocklebur, but he couldn't find a material strong enough to provide the holding power he needed to make a really effective fastener. By sheer coincidence, across the Atlantic in this country, Wallace H. Carouthers of the du Pont Company had just invented a new synthetic fiber that he called nylon. Nylon was tough enough to provide the holding power the Swiss inventor was looking for. The problem was, it was too tough.

Nylon dulled the cutting blades too quickly to allow production runs of the material. It took de Mestral another twenty years to build the proper cutting equipment to produce the material in sufficient quantities to broadly market the hook and loop material he named Velcro—Vel for velvet and Cro for crochet, which is French for hook.

Today, Velcro is replacing zippers and nails for some uses; it's even used to hold on car bumpers and on the bottoms of astronauts' shoes to keep them from floating around in space. And a few years ago, a group of inventors voted Velcro one of the most important inventions of the twentieth century.

De Mestral is proof of Thomas Edison's adage that genius is one percent inspiration and ninety-nine percent perspiration. Next time you have a great idea that doesn't seem to work at first, you may find that if you stick with it, you will eventually prevail.

── POSITIVE ACTION STEPS ──

☞ Don't give up. A good idea may take years to take off.

☞ Set a definite goal.

☞ Work your hardest. Half-efforts yield half-results.

DAY 59

HOW ARE YOU DOING?

A lot of people set goals for themselves. Some even accurately assess where they are at the very beginning and what they need to do to get to their goal. But very few continue to check their progress on a regular basis, and they fall off the path to success.

Sometimes it's a good idea to take inventory of your achievements to measure your progress and to check your direction. Ask yourself the following questions to help identify improvements you could make in your search for success:

1. What is your goal and how far are you from it?

2. Have you set a timetable for reaching your goal with specific steps to complete by specific dates?

3. What role models have you adopted to help give you inspiration and guidance in reaching your goal?

4. What skills, degrees, or other learning experiences have you engaged in to make your task easier?

5. Who have you helped in the last twelve months to reach his or her goals?

6. How many times in the last year have you gone the extra mile in everything you do?

7. What parts of your job do you dislike and how can you minimize those parts?

8. What parts of your job do you like and how can you maximize those?

9. What new business associates have you struck up a friendship with or what old friends have you renewed a friendship with?

10. Do you have a list of written goals for both your business and personal lives that covers at least the next twelve months?

As Napoleon Hill said, "If you don't know where you are going, one direction is as good as another." You must know where you wish to be if you ever have any hope of arriving there.

It doesn't matter where you start from, just that you get started, work hard, and continually check on your progress. One man who understands this better than most is W. Clement Stone.

While some might regard growing up in poverty on Chicago's tough southwest side a real disadvantage, Stone, a self-made millionaire, called it "a blessing." He said, "It taught me to depend on myself, to overcome fear and to work to achieve my goals. Those early lessons became the foundation upon which my success as an adult was built."

His father died when he was very young, leaving young Clement and his mother penniless. Stone attributes much of his own success to his mother's guidance. It was from her that he learned a fundamental principle: Everyone who achieves wealth or outstanding success in any endeavor must set high goals and make sacrifices to achieve them.

Stone first applied the principle at age six, selling newspapers on a busy street corner. When two other newsboys beat him up and drove him away, he refused to give up. Failure simply wasn't an option.

"I had no choice," said Stone. "I borrowed the money to pay for the newspapers. I had to sell them." And he did.

Stone found a nearby restaurant full of people and went inside and sold his papers. Every time the owner kicked him out, he went back in, until his papers were gone.

"What I learned," says Stone, "was the importance of persistence and the right attitude. I also learned that I could sell a lot more than the competition by not being afraid to go where there were large numbers of potential customers."

As a youngster, Stone worked in a variety of jobs before finding his true calling—a career in insurance. Applying the lesson he learned as a newsboy, Stone sought locations that allowed him to see the most customers in the shortest time.

He later learned another useful lesson in a real estate office he called upon. In response to his request for a few minutes of time, the sales manager bellowed: "Young man, as long as you live, when you're selling something don't ask for time. Take it!" That day, instead of the average four policies a day he had been selling, he sold twenty-seven policies in a single stop.

From those humble beginnings, Stone built a multi-billion dollar global insurance empire. When asked what his most important principle of success was, he said, "A positive mental attitude."

—— POSITIVE ACTION STEPS ——

☞ Set daily, weekly, monthly, and yearly,
as well as your ultimate, goals.

☞ Spend time each day thinking about your
ultimate goal, how far you have to go,
and what progress you're making.

☞ Upon reaching a goal, quickly set a new one.

☞ Maintain a positive mental attitude.

DAY 60

BALANCE

To be truly successful, you need to have balance in your life. Success is about doing your best; it's about constant course correction, reaching one plateau and springing to another, and it's about working with others to your mutual advantage. But it's more than these things. Success is also about balance.

Having it all means having a fulfilling career without neglecting everything else that is important. Part of the process of refining and adjusting our goals means that at various times of our lives we have to devote more time to one aspect or another.

Early in our careers, for example, we are building. We work long hours and put in extra effort to earn promotions or to build a clientele or a business. The focus is on money and careers. But problems develop when we become so obsessed with any one aspect of our lives that we neglect other important parts of it.

When we become unbalanced in one part of our lives the imbalance negatively affects our entire life. If we wreck our family relationships or lose all our friends because we spend every waking moment working or worrying about work, we are unsuccessful both at work and at relationships.

The way we view success in our careers is changing. As corporations flatten their hierarchies and fewer middle managers are required to supervise today's workers, a movement is beginning to reward employees based on their knowledge and skill, rather than on their power or number of people they manage. In the future, careers may be built more on horizontal moves rather than the traditional vertical climb toward the top of the corporate ladder.

The goal is to pay people based on their ability to contribute and to learn so they can contribute even more. Which means that more than ever employees need to be more well-balanced, well-rounded individuals. No longer can they keep their heads down, concentrating on just their business. They need to be exposed to the world at large so they can spot trends and get information through various relationships that can help the business adapt to a changing world.

The best way to keep up with what's going on in the world is to read. Become a voracious reader. Read newspapers, magazines, trade journals, and novels. Anything that makes you think will help expand your mind.

One way to achieve this is to read a variety of materials. As a kid, I learned to love reading from my Aunt Hailey. I loved to spend time with her. She was one of the smartest people I knew and she was always up on what was going on in the world. She didn't have a television, but she did have lots of magazines and books. Because of her, I learned the joys of reading and learning—not the dull stuff we were required to read for school, but inspirational stories about great adventures and great people in history and about travel to faraway places. Of course, I didn't realize it at the time, but it was she who helped me discover the power of thought.

It is one of the great ironies of our time that as more and more of us are becoming so-called "knowledge workers," we seem to have less and less time to read, think, study, and reflect—the very things that allow us to transform the vast amounts of information available to us into knowledge. Sure, it takes a lot less effort to watch a video, but as a neurosurgeon I know once pointed out, there is no thought or creativity involved in watching what someone else has done. That is about as effective as trying to get into shape by watching someone else exercise.

Just as you gain strength from exercise, you gain knowledge by reading, studying, analyzing, and reflecting upon the information you've gathered. And knowledgeable people—who take action to put their knowledge to practical use—are always the leaders of the pack in any occupation, business, or profession.

Make sure you take a little time every day to read and reflect upon the things that are important to you. When you become a reader, it follows automatically that you will become a thinker. And being a thinker will help you maintain your competitive edge.

My Aunt Hailey is in her 70s now and is still as knowledgeable and interesting as ever. She still doesn't have a TV, but she does have lots of books and magazines. There could be a connection.

—— POSITIVE ACTION STEPS ——

☞ Allow at least one-half hour each day
to read, study, and reflect.

☞ Combining exercise with reflection time is a
good way to keep mentally and physically fit.

☞ Read to your kids. It's good for both of you.

DAY 61

PSYCHOLOGY OF SUCCESS

D r. Ilona Tobin, a psychologist who practices in the upscale Detroit suburb of Birmingham, Michigan, uses a mix of classic psychological techniques, the logic of the great philosophers, and the proven principles of success to help her patients solve their problems. "I have found that the only way to get through the intellectual defenses of my well-educated, affluent clients is to keep it simple," she says.

She explains her approach this way: "Think of a beautiful Sunday morning where a little boy is looking forward to seeing his father and spending time with him. The father, on the other hand, is looking forward to doing nothing—just kicking back and relaxing. He's just leaned back in his favorite chair to read the Sunday comics when his son comes up and says, 'Dad, I'm ready. Today is Sunday. You promised.'

"To buy a little time, the father rips a puzzle out of the paper and sends his son away to solve it. The boy is back almost immediately with the problem solved and the father says, 'How did you do that so quickly? I gave you a picture of the world to put together. You don't know anything about the world.'

"The boy says, 'Yeah, but if you flip it over, there's a man on the back. If you put the man together, the world falls into place.'"

You have to put yourself together before your world will fall into place. But only you can make it happen. "You have dreams," Dr. Tobin says. "What are you willing to do to make them come true? If you just sit around and complain, nothing is going to happen. You have to get into action, to do something. Otherwise your dreams are nothing more than wishful thinking."

One person who would agree with this assessment is Steve Thomas, the personable host of the PBS program *This Old House*. "I'm an advocate of dreaming big, and then pursuing your dreams," he says.

"A lot of people defeat themselves by not reaching high enough. Such people say, 'I could never do that.' But they could do a lot more than they think if they only try. As the saying goes, 'Fortune smiles on the bold.'"

Thomas' career is a study in reaching for the stars. After he graduated from Evergreen State College in Olympia, Washington, he supported himself mostly by renovating houses and working as a construction foreman. But his first love was sailing.

He raced rebuilt sailboats from the West Coast to Hawaii and captained a yacht from England to San Francisco when he was only twenty-five years old. It was during one of those races that he became interested in the South Sea Islanders who for the past six thousand years have sailed the Pacific using only natural signs—stars, waves, and birds—to guide them.

He spent two years as the apprentice of a Micronesian sailor, and learned the secrets of navigation never before taught to a westerner. He wrote a book about his sailing adventures called *The Last Navigator* and narrated a public television episode about it for the Boston station that produces *This Old House*.

He was in the middle of renovating his own old house when the producer discovered his construction skills and gift of gab. She persuaded him to try out for the job as host of the show.

"It wasn't what I had planned for my life," Thomas told me, "but I have found that when I focus on my next step, whatever it is, the process develops a logic of its own. Another path may present itself to you, so you pursue that one. As long as you are flexible and alert to the opportunity that is around you all the time, it will come to you."

Thomas' yardstick for success comes in the answer to a question posed by one of his college professors: "If you knew you were going to die in six months, would you be doing what you're doing right now?"

"If not," Thomas says, "why on earth are you doing it now?"

—— POSITIVE ACTION STEPS ——

☞ Write down all your wishes on a piece of paper.

☞ Rank your wishes in order of importance to you.

☞ Take definite action toward fulfilling your top wish.

DAY 62

YOU CAN'T HAVE EVERYTHING

Several years ago, I had the opportunity to meet the great Earl Nightingale, whose radio broadcasts and recordings have inspired millions of listeners over the years. Although he was getting on in years and in poor health at the time, he still had the magic. I've never forgotten his words that day, delivered in his own inimitable style and voice. He said: "There is nothing in this world that you cannot have in five years' time if you are willing to pay the price for it."

Think about it. Anything can be yours in just five years if you are willing to do what's necessary to get it. If you imagine yourself in the house of your dreams or at the controls of your own airplane, you can have either. As you read these words, you know you can have them.

Already you are thinking of what you would have to give up and the steps you would have to take to achieve those goals. You would have to save enough for a down payment, maintain a good credit rating, cut back on other expenses, make more money, get a pilot's license—but all of those things are possible and doable if that's the thing you want more than anything else in the world.

The difficulty lies not in achieving a goal once you've set it for yourself; the difficulty lies in deciding which goal is more important. We are all faced with an endless array of needs and wants and desires, most of which are attainable. However, it is not likely that they are all attainable at the same time. Success requires focus, priorities, and determination bordering on obsession. The good news is that success in one area often makes success in other areas possible later on.

For instance, if you do everything that is necessary to acquire your own airplane, you've increased your earning potential and upped your credit rating. These are positive steps that could help you with your next goal—a bigger house, or a fancy sports car, or providing for a family. Often the steps toward one goal also bring you closer to others.

But to achieve any of them you must first focus exclusively on one until you achieve it. Then you can turn to others, and you may be surprised to discover that you are now a lot closer to them than you were before.

Of course, all the dreams in the world won't get you where you want to be unless you take the initiative to make at least one thing happen.

One person who put this strategy into action is Amy Hilliard-Jones. A marketing strategist at the Gillette Company, Hilliard-Jones saw an opportunity in White Rain Shampoo, a product that at the time the company was considering dropping because it wasn't selling as it should. It wasn't a pricing problem; White Rain was positioned as an inexpensive, no-frills shampoo that should have appealed to cost-conscious consumers.

But it didn't.

As the story is told in the book, *Napoleon Hill's Keys to Success,* Hilliard-Jones developed a campaign to reposition the shampoo as a high quality, value-added product for executives.

Her strategy worked, and White Rain became one of Gillette's best-selling products.

Because she had achieved such remarkable success with a failing product, the company recognized that Hilliard-Jones was an ideal candidate to head up the effort to revitalize the Lustrasilk Corporation, a newly acquired Gillette subsidary that targeted the ethnic hair care market.

Building on that opportunity, she created a whole new product line—Moisture Max—which was phenomenally successful.

Today, Hilliard-Jones is executive vice-president of Burrell Communications Group, a specialty marketing company which helps Fortune 500 companies sell their products and services to African Americans. She got where she is because she always took the initiative to make something happen. Each success put her in a position to excel at even higher levels.

The companies she worked for recognized her ability, her dedication, and her desire to make things happen, and so did the Harvard Business School, which gave her the Max and Cohen Award for Excellence in Retailing. And recently *Dollars & Sense* magazine named her one of the "Top Business and Professional Women" in America.

Personal initiative paid off for Amy Hilliard-Jones in recognition, advancement, and the opportunity to do exactly what she wanted in her career. By disciplining herself to reach one goal, she helped herself to eventually reach her ultimate goal. You can do the same.

— POSITIVE ACTION STEPS —

☞ Determine what you wish to attain and what
you might be willing to give up in exchange.

☞ Concentrate on one goal at a time.
Reach it, then move on to the next.

☞ Sticking to your goal until you achieve it will
help you develop the determination and
focus to achieve all your future goals.

DAY 63

NEW OUTLETS

Your job is repetitive and boring. There's no room for creativity in your daily routine. One way to deal with it is to find new outlets outside your job.

Many people who work in repetitive jobs become leaders in church, school, or civic affairs or part-time painters or musicians. Often, their managers and co-workers have no idea about the responsible positions these people hold outside of work.

To break the ice in company-sponsored workshops and seminars, I frequently ask participants to get acquainted with a person in the group that they don't normally work with, then introduce the person to the group. They can use any speaking style they wish, or they may tell us anything about the person that the individual is willing to share. The only criterion is: Make that person interesting to the rest of the group. Tell us something different or unusual about him or her. Don't tell us their titles or positions; we already know that.

There is always a surprise or two when people reveal their personal achievements to people with whom they do not ordinarily talk about such things. It electrifies the entire group on those occasions when, for example, an executive realizes that a secretary (whom he has for years treated like a child) in her spare time has a responsible position on a board of directors or is active in a civic group charged with the oversight of a large organization.

Ordinary people do amazing things when they are allowed to do so. For years, philosophers have debated whether great events make great people or if ordinary people rise to greatness when the situation demands it.

There may be some truth to both theories, but time and time again when we see people on the evening news who have risked their lives to save someone else's they say, "It was nothing that anyone else wouldn't have done under the same circumstances." Perhaps that's their way of saying that we all have within ourselves the potential for greatness, but we don't challenge ourselves as we should. It takes an unexpected event or crisis to demand that we face up to our potential.

If we would just realize that we are capable of greatness and have the faith in ourselves to try, the world could become an incredible place.

It's true that having faith that you can accomplish something will not automatically cause you to achieve your objective, but it will give you the courage to do what you must to reach your goal. Faith may not bring you what you want, but without it you would never begin anything worthwhile.

There will be times in your life when you cannot prove that your faith in yourself is justified. You must accept as fact your intuitive inner feelings that you are capable of greatness. No doubt you will be disappointed in yourself when you fail to live up to your expectations. If you don't have faith in yourself, however, you will never begin to reach your potential because you will be unwilling to try.

Once you begin to have faith in yourself, you'll find a wonderful thing will happen. You will subconsciously begin to act with more confidence and enthusiasm. Others will respond in kind.

Their faith in you will soon grow to the point where they may begin to entrust you with new projects and opportunities. And you, of course, will have the faith in yourself to accept these new opportunities.

To build your faith in yourself, think about all the things at which you excel and the areas in which you know you could excel if just given the chance. Develop motivational phrases like "I can do it" and "I can accomplish anything I set my mind to" and repeat them aloud twenty times in the morning and twenty times before you go to bed. Constant repetition will cause you to believe that these things really are true. (Advertising works on the same principle.) Planting these thoughts firmly into your subconscious will cause you to act in a more confident manner in everything you do.

You really can achieve any goal you set for yourself with a little faith and a lot of hard work.

—— POSITIVE ACTION STEPS ——

☞ If you do not utilize your full potential on the job, find a way to exercise it on the outside—or soon your potential will begin to shrink and disappear.

☞ Utilizing your potential outside work can help you make contacts which can help you find a more challenging job.

☞ Squelch self-doubt with work. Hard work will help you succeed, worry will not.

CHAPTER TEN

A GOOD ORGANIZATION

Organization can make a big improvement in almost every facet of our lives. Week Ten focuses on organizing and incorporating success, health, and well-being principles into our everyday lives.

DAY 64

THE POWER OF ORGANIZATION

Earl Nightingale once said, "Ideas are like slippery fish. Unless you gaffe them on the point of a pencil, they are likely to get away."

No doubt you've had a "Eureka!" experience of your own when an idea came to you that was nothing short of brilliant, and a few days later it was long forgotten. Advertising executive Chuck Frey offers these tips on how to retain and organize those good ideas so they can be put to good use later when the time is right. He offers three methods.

The first is to use a pocket-sized notepad. A number of companies manufacture leather index card holders; some companies even give them away as premiums. The holders will easily accommodate a modest supply of three-by-five index cards that you can conveniently carry in your suit pocket, briefcase, or purse. When you get an idea, jot down the key points and convert them to a more permanent form by typing them into your computer or word processor once a week or writing them in your journal or daily planner.

The second method Frey recommends is a microcassette recorder. With today's electronics, these tiny recorders can be easily carried in your pocket and offer excellent sound quality when you replay the ideas you've dictated to be transcribed for permanent storage. Handwriting and typing force you to slow your brain to the speed of your hands, but you can dictate as fast as you can talk. This may help keep the creative flow going.

The third method is even more high tech. It's called a personal digital assistant, it's tiny, and some brands even come with a rudimentary word processor that allows you to record your thoughts and ideas while they are fresh in your mind. At your convenience, you can transfer the information to your computer so the data can be quickly searched for key words.

Frey suggests trying all three methods to see which works for you. The key is to record those good ideas when they strike. That thought that awakens you in the middle of the night may be genius calling. But you'll never know if you don't retain the idea for future use.

The next step is organize your ideas. Getting organized is critical to making your ideas pay off and reaching your goals. There are few of us who will not benefit from organization, and nothing bolsters self-confidence like the knowledge that you understand the job that needs to be done and have organized it in a sensible, logical fashion.

Some people are list makers; others use daily planners, pocket computers, or one of many commercially available systems designed to help you get your life in order. There are numerous tools available to you; all you need to furnish are the desire and the discipline.

The first step is to plan your work. Make it a practice to stop and think about the task at hand before you jump in and start. If you take the time to think about a job at the beginning, you will complete it far more efficiently.

Organization is a great time saver, and it allows you to focus on larger issues rather than struggling to complete routine tasks. If you make personal organization a critical component of your success philosophy, you will be more confident, which will enable you to achieve more.

Being organized also relieves stress. If you write down your goals and have a plan for achieving them, you don't have to keep worrying about them, fearing that you might forget something.

The engine that drives organization is personal discipline. It is the willpower, the determination, the strength of character that compels you to stay with the job until it is finished. Unfortunately, there is no easy way to develop personal discipline. It's the result of forcing yourself to do the right thing, to take the initiative to accomplish something when you'd much rather be doing something else.

Personal discipline is developed one act and one day at a time until it becomes a habit. Soon you'll automatically act on your inner voice when it tells you to get going and take positive action instead of procrastinating. It's all up to you. Personal discipline allows you to ignore the criticism of others and to stop blaming your heritage, your environment, bad luck, or other people for your situation. It allows you to recognize that you have had problems, and who doesn't, but you can and will overcome them.

In all the world, you are the only person who is ultimately responsible for your successes, your failures, and your happiness. So the next time you say to yourself, "I really need to get organized," first realize that you're right, then take some action to do it. It's up to you to take charge of your life.

—— POSITIVE ACTION STEPS ——

☞ Organize your day to reduce stress.

☞ Force yourself to stick with your organizational
plan until it becomes automatic.

☞ Ideas can be fleeting—write them down.

DAY 65

BUDGETING TIME AND MONEY

John Wanamaker, the Philadelphia merchant king, once said of budgeting one's time and resources, "The man who doesn't have a fixed system for the use of his time and money will never have financial security, unless he has a rich relative who leaves him a fortune."

Professional people like doctors, lawyers, accountants, and consultants are keenly aware that time is the only thing they have to sell. So they develop a system of accounting for their time—an hourly rate that covers the cost of doing business and builds in a profit.

It's a lesson for us all; time is our greatest asset. It is the one asset we possess that can be converted into any form of wealth we choose. You can spend your time wisely, or you can squander it and spend your entire life without a purpose beyond securing food and shelter.

Benjamin Franklin is said to have advised that if you love life, "then do not squander time, for that's the stuff that life is made of."

The average person's time can be divided into three parts: sleep, work, and recreation. But it is your recreation time that is the most important as far as your personal achievement is concerned. Your free time provides you with the opportunity for self-improvement and education which, in turn, will allow you to market your work time for a right price. The person who uses all his or her free time solely for personal pleasure and play will never be a great success at anything.

It is vital to allow yourself time for creative thought. A good starting point is to devote a half hour each day solely to creative thinking. The time of day depends on the individual; some people think more clearly during morning walks; others prefer a quiet time just before going to sleep at night. Experiment with your own rhythms to determine when you do your best thinking, then reserve that time every day for creative thinking without any distractions.

Truly successful people also budget the income and outgo of their money as carefully as they budget their time. A definite amount is set aside for food, clothing, household expenses, for savings and investment, for charity, and for recreation. Naturally, individual circumstances vary, and specific amounts allocated to each will depend on your occupation and earning ability.

Personal savings and investments are frequently areas that are neglected when other expenses increase, but there is an often overlooked side benefit of saving. In times of emergency, even a modest bank account can give you courage and security; in times of prosperity, it will bolster your self-confidence and reduce anxiety. Worry over money matters can kill your ambition—and you.

One of the best ways to set aside money for investment and savings is by following the "ten percent rule." Simply stated, you set aside ten percent of each paycheck right off the top—before you pay any other bills. By paying yourself first, you insure that you will have enough money to set aside. If you pay yourself last, it's too easy to spend that money on something else.

Ten percent may sound like a lot, but if you are an impulsive buyer or spendthrift, believe me, you will never even miss it. If your employer has direct deposit, see if you can have ten percent of your check deposited into a separate account that you never touch. If you are tempted to dig into that money after it really starts to build, remind yourself that it is for a new house, retirement, or your safety cushion. Don't even pay bills with it. This is attitude money. You can weather a lot of ups and downs if you know you can pay off your bills, but choose not to, preferring cash rather than paid bills when another crisis comes along.

As with most other goals in life, you have to make it happen for yourself. Don't count on Social Security or your pension plan. They may not come through. Count on yourself. Spend your money wisely, and put away at least ten percent for later. Don't let life get the best of you; plan to get the best out of life. Take time to budget your time and your money.

—— POSITIVE ACTION STEPS ——

☞ Set aside a half hour each day for creative thinking.

☞ Set aside ten percent of your earnings
for saving and investment.

☞ Use some of your free time to
study success principles.

DAY 66

PRACTICE GOOD HABITS

In your life, you can help attract success by making sure that you set aside time to study, think, and plan. Work smarter, not harder—intelligently balance your use of time and your business and personal resources.

We all have the same twenty-four hours in each day. Your day is divided into time for sleep, time for work, and time for recreation and spare time activities. Make sure you allow time for each, that you live a balanced life. Remember the old adage: everything in moderation. Working too much can be as detrimental to your long-term financial and personal success as working too little.

Budget your financial resources with care as well. Make one dollar do the work of two. Set aside a portion of your income for emergencies, and invest in your future. Budget for personal growth, plan for long-range expenses, such as a college education for your kids and your retirement. When you invest, practice the other principles of success, especially definiteness of purpose, accurate thinking, self-discipline, and a positive mental attitude.

Be willing to start right from where you are. Just because you were born with disadvantages doesn't mean you can't overcome them. As Napoleon Hill pointed out, perhaps the worst thing that might have happened to you would be to have been born with the proverbial silver spoon in your mouth. Had you been born into privilege, you would have been deprived of one of the world's greatest gifts—the opportunity to reach the highest levels of success of which you are capable—solely on the basis of your own merit.

When every opportunity is a step up, the rewards are far greater than when the reverse is true. If you were born with less than most, don't resent others who seem to have more advantages. In truth, the real advantage is yours, for you will develop the self-confidence that comes only from meeting life's challenges on your own terms.

As you progress, you gain the strength and knowledge necessary to assure your enduring success, things that cannot be given to you—they must be earned.

The source of this new strength is the faith in yourself that comes from overcoming setbacks. We all make mistakes every day, but we don't let them get to us. We find the problems and fix them. By overcoming small defeats, we learn the skills to overcome the big ones that we all experience.

Even temporary defeat can help us later on. Every problem you solve, every setback you overcome helps bring you one step closer to your ultimate goal.

If you try to think about all the possible problems you may encounter along the way, you may never start. There is no reason to worry about problems that haven't even happened.

The late Dr. Kenneth McFarland, one of the greatest speakers who ever lived, once likened life to an automobile trip. If you think about the danger of taking a long trip, he said, if you think about all those other cars speeding by just inches away, you would never have the courage to leave home.

Fortunately, we don't live life that way. We go little by little, a mile at a time, and a day at a time.

That's also the best way to deal with setbacks—one at a time as they come up. And if you learn from each experience, you won't have to make the same mistake twice.

By making it a habit to face up to setbacks, you have taken another important step toward lasting success.

—— POSITIVE ACTION STEPS ——

☞ Strive to live a balanced life. Work, study, and recreation are all important components of success.

☞ Budget for today, but be sure to invest for the future.

☞ Have faith in yourself and your ability to overcome setbacks.

DAY 67

MAINTAINING SOUND PHYSICAL AND MENTAL HEALTH

To maintain both your physical and mental health, strive to live a balanced life. Work, play, rest, nourishment, exercise, and study are all important to your overall well-being. Maintain a positive mental attitude in all you do. Never stop learning, be enthusiastic, have faith in yourself, and work to achieve your goals from a well-thought-out plan.

At work, get organized. A written agenda not only helps you be more efficient with your time, it also reduces the stress that you might forget something. Work your hardest and always try to go that extra mile for your boss and customers, but don't spend all your time working. All work and no play not only makes Jack a dull boy, eventually it makes him a sick boy too.

Recreation and play are important to relieve tension and help your body recuperate. Play also helps your mind shift gears and gain a different perspective, which can help you find more creative solutions to your problems. Rest is an absolute requirement to maintain your physical and mental health. Your body tells you when it's time to rest. Listen to it.

Proper nourishment is very important to your well-being. The old saw that "you are what you eat" is true. A diet low in fat, high in fiber, and with plenty of fresh fruits and vegetables will not only do wonders for your waistline, but you may be pleasantly surprised at how it improves your powers of concentration and memory.

Exercise is not just for the body. Improved blood flow and circulation from exercise mean the brain is better supplied with oxygen and the other nutrients it needs to function. A half hour a day of vigorous cardiovascular exercise like jogging or brisk walking will help keep your body in tune. (Of course, more exercise is needed to tone your muscles or lose significant amounts of weight.) Recent research shows that walking has a cumulative effect. Three ten-minute walks are just as good for you as one half-hour walk.

Controlling your environment in the home or office can also help keep you healthy. You already know that low humidity can cause dry, itchy eyes and skin, but it can be worse.

Prevention magazine publishers cite *Body Bulletin*, which recently reported that relative humidity below thirty percent (normal in many large, centrally heated and air-conditioned office buildings) can irritate nasal and bronchial airways. The result: lowered resistance to infection, which leads to a common cold or worse.

If you can't control the humidity, *Prevention* suggests keeping plants in your office. The large-leafed ones are especially good contributors to the moisture content in the air.

The magazine also offers some other, more novel tips for warding off sickness:

- ☞ Wash your hands frequently. Germs travel better by touch than by air. Handshakes can be infectious.

☞ Cry if you feel like it (or anything else that helps you relieve stress). Too much stress lowers immunity to a host of diseases, including the common cold.

☞ Grow a beard. Yes, the editors promise that facial hair (especially around the nose and mouth) can act as a cold-virus filter.

Well, it can't hurt. Scientists have finally admitted that grandma's chicken soup really does have cold-fighting properties. Who's to say that crying in your whiskers won't be next to win acclaim.

Don't forget study and reflection. These are perhaps the most important things you can do for your mental well-being. Study feeds the mind and expands it. Quiet reflection gives your mind a chance to get things into perspective.

Strive to live a balanced life, to do everything in moderation. Follow work with play, mental effort with physical, eating with fasting, seriousness with humor, and you will be on your way to sound health and happiness.

—— POSITIVE ACTION STEPS ——

☞ Exercise at least a half hour each day.

☞ Cut fat from your diet.

☞ Organize your workday, and be sure to leave time for study and reflection.

DAY 68

THE POWER OF INFORMATION

Futurist and best-selling author Alvin Toffler called it *The Third Wave*, and wrote a book with that title. The book was about the revolutionary changes in our society that are being driven by the rapid advances in technology that are occurring all around us.

He wrote that the first wave of transforming change in human history was the agricultural revolution of ten thousand years ago; the second wave was the industrial revolution of the seventeen and eighteen hundreds. The third wave, he figures, began in the mid-1950s as computers and other high-tech gadgetry began to make their mark on society. Today, decades later, we are in the middle of the information age.

Computers are used for everything from making movies to calculating the age of the universe, and their use is spreading so quickly that it's hard to keep up with the numbers. If you haven't yet joined the information age, don't waste another minute becoming computer literate. Buy yourself a personal computer if you can afford it, take an adult education class, or go to a library—whatever you need to do to learn. Every day you delay just puts you one step further behind.

The New York Times recently reported, "For all but the most skilled or best educated new workers, wages and hours are the stingiest since President Franklin D. Roosevelt created the welfare system."

Once powerful unions, which could help members learn new skills, represent half the number of workers they did just twenty years ago. It's not much better in white-collar jobs. Computers have helped eliminate whole layers of middle management. They have also created a system that makes it possible to do your work at any time of the day or night, and transmit it electronically to any destination around the globe.

We are squarely in the middle of an information explosion. When the phrase *knowledge is power* was coined, the challenge was digging up information. With today's technology, the challenge isn't finding the information, it's knowing what to do with it.

Figuring out what all that information means to us requires constant reading and studying. Set aside time each day—preferably the same time each day—to read the newspaper, a trade magazine, or a good book, or all three online. Seek variety in your reading to help expand your mind.

Train yourself to retain information that is of value to you. Make notes. Clip articles. Don't attempt to retain everything; let go of everything that does not in some way affect you.

You can also improve yourself in this information age by turning off the TV. Instead, spend that time watching training or motivational videos. Listen to podcasts during commuting or any time you're trapped in a car to expand your productive time.

As you study, watch for the unusual, the anomalies, the things that surprise you in light of everything you already know. Look for patterns and events that affect more than one industry or geographic area of the country. A new idea or fad is well on its way to becoming a trend when it begins to cross industry or geographic lines. Recognition of trends can create great opportunities. The earlier you recognize them, the more chance you have of capitalizing on these opportunities.

W. Clement Stone labeled this technique the "R2A2 principle," which stands for recognize, relate, assimilate, and apply information from any field that will help you achieve your goals, whatever they may be. The key to opportunity can be anywhere. Be alert for information you can use, regardless of the source.

If you have clearly defined your goals, your mind will almost automatically sift the information you expose it to and help you sort out those pieces of information that will help you reach your goals. Keep in mind, however, there is no shortcut for reading and studying. You have to put in your time every day, but the more you practice these principles, the better you become at identifying trends and finding information that can help you achieve success in the information age.

── POSITIVE ACTION STEPS ──

☞ Endeavor to read a wide variety of subject matter.

☞ Listen to learning and motivational
tapes while commuting.

☞ Look for patterns and trends in your reading—
they may point to future opportunities.

DAY 69

CAPITALIZING ON CHANGE

I t was the ancient Roman philosopher Pliny the Elder who was first to observe that the only permanent thing in life is change. We humans have known for thousands of years that we live in a world of change, yet we still resist it.

W. Clement Stone observed that in today's rapidly changing world, your happiness and success depend upon how you meet the challenge of change. But how you meet the challenge of change depends on how you meet the challenge to change.

When Richard Nixon passed away, Henry Kissinger delivered a eulogy at the former president's burial. About the controversial Nixon, he said, "So let us now say good-bye to our gallant friend. He stood on pinnacles that dissolved and he suffered deeply, but he never gave up."

Stone says, "I can think of no finer tribute to a man who left the presidency in disgrace, yet became one of America's most respected elder statesmen."

Nixon's political career is a study in learning to meet the challenge of change. When he lost the California governor's race and said: "You're not going to have Dick Nixon to kick around anymore," many thought the main reason he lost was because of exactly that kind of emotional immaturity.

No doubt you've heard Nixon's line, but you may not be quite so familiar with what happened afterward. He set out to change himself, to change his attitude from negative to positive. He spent time studying, thinking, and planning, and he engaged in long bouts of soul searching. He read inspirational self-help books and magazines. He moved to New York and became head of one of America's top law firms. He attended services at New York's Marble Collegiate Church and was inspired by the positive messages of Dr. Norman Vincent Peale. He was elected Chairman of the Board of Directors of the Boys' Clubs of America and by helping hundreds of thousands of disadvantaged boys throughout America, Nixon himself developed inner strength.

It was precisely that inner strength that enabled him to return to politics and be elected president of the United States. It also allowed him to overcome the disgrace and despair of his resignation and become a noted author and analyst of world affairs.

Dealing with change in the business world takes just as much dedication, hard work, and determination as it does in personal life. Gone are the days when managers could simply set goals, formulate strategies, and implement programs to achieve success. With declining productivity and competitiveness, managers must learn to not just react to change, but to anticipate and embrace it.

One way to create a dynamic, change-oriented organization is to develop the ability to spot trends, ask the right questions, and to get to the heart of a problem and deal with it—instead of just treating the symptoms.

By discerning trends in related fields you can implement change when it's needed instead of merely reacting to it and playing catch-up. Expose yourself to a wide range of information.

Newspapers, trade journals, magazines—the more widely read you are, the better the chances are that you will spot trends that can affect your business.

Once you identify a trend, you must have the courage and determination to make a change and exploit it. You must develop confidence in yourself and your idea and be sensitive to the fears of others. But you must act. If you don't, you will eventually have to react, and you will join the ranks of the also-rans who are doomed to play catch-up.

Change is constant. This means you must constantly look for ways to make it work for you. Embrace change, and unlimited opportunity is yours. Ignore change, and soon you and your company will be ignored.

—— POSITIVE ACTION STEPS ——

☞ Change is constant. Constantly search for creative ways to anticipate and react to change.

☞ Change brings opportunity—welcome change and you welcome opportunity. Resist change and you are doomed to fail.

☞ Be willing to adopt and innovate. What worked yesterday may not work today.

DAY 70

OLD OR NEW

Any goal that you set for yourself can be achieved by applying proven success principles. W. Clement Stone offers this series of definite steps to help you achieve your objective.

Set aside time for thought, planning, and study. Choose a time and place that works best for you and make it a practice to use this time to identify principles that will help you achieve your goals. Write down your goals so you can review them to check on your progress. Make adjustments and corrections, as necessary, and concentrate every day for an entire week on a specific goal before proceeding to the next, leaving the previous one to the function of the subconscious mind.

By reviewing and inspecting your written goals daily, you will recall through the suggestion of the written word those goals toward which you are making progress and those you are not.

Of course, these steps work only if you work. Only you can write down and review your goals daily, and set aside time to plan and identify principles that can help you reach your goals. Stone asks, "Do you really want to change or do you prefer a continuation of the old you, with negative habits of thought, apathy, and inaction which may have brought you and your loved ones unhappiness, miseries, sickness, and failure? Or do you prefer a new you with a more positive mental attitude with habits, thoughts, and actions in which you adopt the self-motivating philosophy of *do it now?*

Here are some tips you can use to help keep yourself on track.

First, set a definite timetable for reaching your goal. Without a deadline, it's easy to put off difficult tasks.

Never give up. Don't let adversity and minor setbacks keep you from reaching your goal. We all make mistakes and experience difficulties, but none are great enough to keep you from achieving greatness.

Go public with your goal. Telling others what you wish to accomplish makes it too embarrassing to quit.

Finally, break down large goals into smaller steps so you can see how you can go about accomplishing your objectives. Map out what you will achieve each month for the next year.

It's up to you. You must take control—of your mind, your emotions, and your actions. In short, you must develop self-discipline.

Self-discipline becomes easier with practice. If you get in the habit of accomplishing the goals you set for yourself, according to your predetermined schedule, success will follow.

—— POSITIVE ACTION STEPS ——

☞ Set aside time each day to study success principles.

☞ Write down your goals and review them daily.

☞ Adopt the motivator "do it now"
to avoid procrastination.

CHAPTER ELEVEN

TAKING CARE OF BUSINESS

Roughly one-third of our lives is spent at work or pursuing work. This week focuses on both practical and success-oriented tips on working, selling, and making yourself more marketable.

DAY 71

WORKING AT HOME

Recently, I attended a ribbon-cutting ceremony in Knoxville, Tennessee, dedicating the new building that houses the Home and Garden Cable TV network. A friend of mine who works there invited me down for the festivities, and he gave me a grand tour of the facility.

One of the things that impressed me most, something that I think will profoundly influence the way we work in the future, was that the technology is such today that several people can work at the same time on animated visuals that will be bounced off a satellite and available for you to watch in the comfort of your easy chair at home. A supervisor can monitor several screens simultaneously and tell how each computer artist is doing on the work he or she is performing. They don't have to be in the same room; they don't even have to be in the same building. With today's technology, it is possible for you to work on your computer at home and transmit your work back and forth for review and revision.

It struck me that in this kind of environment, it will no longer be possible to escape responsibility for our actions—or inaction. Those folks whose greatest skill seems to be talking their way out of problems or explaining how they had the project finished but the dog ate the paper just before it was turned in, will have no place to hide in the high-tech world we will all be working in soon.

If you haven't already taken the steps learn the skills you will need in the future, you'd better get started. If you don't, you can be sure you will soon be left in the cosmic dust in cyberspace.

In the electronic networks of the future, our work is going to be out there for everyone to see. It will quickly be apparent who is performing at high levels and who isn't.

If you currently work at home or are considering this alternative, here are some tips for maximizing your effectiveness.

First, make sure you have a dedicated work space. It can be a room converted to an office or a desk in the corner of the bedroom—the important thing is that it is used exclusively for work. This allows you to avoid the urge to procrastinate when getting started each day.

Next, talk to other at-home workers. Learn from their experience what works and what doesn't. Ask them about the best support services—printers, mailing services, answering services, and the like, as well as professionals like attorneys and accountants who specialize in small businesses.

Be sure to keep regular office hours. Part of the charm of working at home is the flexibility to work at times that are best for you, but remember that your clients and customers are more attuned to a nine-to-five workday. Make sure that your schedule includes at least a few hours during conventional working hours.

Other tips include using hotels or luncheon clubs for meetings with groups that are too large for your home office or for those you wish to particularly impress. Also be sure to take advantage of publications and consultation services available from companies that specialize in serving home-based businesses. AT&T, for example, has a number of publications and consultants who can help you with 800 lines, faxes, modems, answering services, and a number of related services.

Next, make sure your insurance is adequate. Protecting computers, furniture, and equipment and additional liability exposure may require more insurance. Talk your new situation over with your agent and make sure you are covered.

Your home office may even be tax deductible. Have your accountant check into the requirements your home office must meet.

Finally, whether you're working at home or at the office, the same rules of success apply: Set goals, work hard, and be fair and honest in all your dealings.

If you are not currently a "telecommuter," chances are good that you soon will be. With computers, modems, and fax machines, workers can easily be linked to company offices, clients, suppliers, and others with whom they need to communicate.

"Telecommuting" allows greater flexibility in working hours and allows home-based workers to avoid wasting time in traffic. In addition, the savings realized from the limited office space and support staff needed make telecommuting an attractive alternative to employers as well.

—— POSITIVE ACTION STEPS ——

☞ Set aside a separate specific work space.

☞ Set up a work schedule—and stick with it.

☞ Talk to others who work at home to get helpful tips.

DAY 72

THE POWER OF ACTION

You have a bit of magic inside you, according to W. Clement Stone. You can prove it to yourself when you learn, understand, and follow through with action to apply the self-help principles learned from what you read, experience, see, or hear.

Action is the key word. Whatever you would like to achieve in life, you can do so, Stone says, if you learn to recognize, relate, assimilate, and apply the proven principles of success in your own life. You can use the principles that all great achievers have followed if you really want to.

Spend time every day thinking about specific goals and objectives you would like to achieve.

Write down your goals and make it a habit every day to review your progress. Use simple charts and graphs to compare your actual achievements to your plan. This system works particularly well with financial and sales goals, but virtually any activity can be charted.

Something amazing will happen to you when you truly understand the words and concepts behind the principles of success. You will find that they will work just as well for you as they have for thousands of other achievers.

Finally—and most important—Stone advises, react to the concepts you read in self-help motivational materials by applying the techniques and principles in your own life. Remember:

action is the magic word! All the thinking in the world won't do any good unless you do something with the knowledge you've accumulated.

Thomas Edison once observed that the reason most folks don't recognize opportunity when it comes knocking is that it is usually dressed in coveralls and looks like work. The great inventor was obsessive when it came to his work in the laboratory. In order to spend more time at work, he conditioned himself to get by on four or five hours of sleep a night. He did this by taking short naps during the day.

They were very short naps, indeed. He would rest his head on his desk while holding a metal object such as a ball bearing or a set of keys in his hand. Underneath was a metal pan. When he relaxed sufficiently to drop the object, the noise it made when it hit the pan woke him up.

He credited his breakthrough with the electric light to one of those naps. He had tried and failed more than ten thousand times and was no closer to his objective when, during a short nap, he dreamed about charcoal. When he awoke, he realized that the solution to his problem had come to him in the dream.

Charcoal is made by limiting the supply of oxygen to a wood fire, which keeps it from burning up. If he could apply the same principle to his electric light, he might be able to make it work. So he took a glass jar, put a filament in it, and pumped out the air. The rest, of course, is history. Without oxygen, the filament couldn't burn up as it had in those ten thousand previous experiments.

At the time, the technique of making charcoal was widely known. So was the knowledge that when electricity was sent through a wire it would glow. The great Edison simply combined these two well-known facts and applied the knowledge in a different way, and in the process, he changed the course of civilization.

The next time you awaken from a deep sleep thinking about a dream that seems to make no sense at the time, don't discount it too quickly. It may be your subconscious mind telling you that it has found the answer to a problem with which you've been wrestling.

—— POSITIVE ACTION STEPS ——

☞ Adopt "do it now" as a motivator to action.

☞ Make "to do" lists of what you need to accomplish to further your success—and set about doing it—now!

☞ Ideas can be fleeting. Next time you have a flash of brilliance, write it down so you can act on it later.

DAY 73

SELLING THE VALUE
OF YOUR SERVICES

In today's crowded marketplace, there are so many products that many appear virtually identical. More and more, products seem to all have the same quality and relative value. So how do you sell your product over another? By selling yourself with the product.

You can gain the competitive edge—even if you're selling a commodity product—by focusing on the value-added services that you offer. Here are some tips on how you can differentiate yourself and your company from the competition.

First, determine where you are providing value. Why do customers do business with you? What is special about you, your company, or your product?

Next, check the competition. Analyze competitors' strong points and where they are vulnerable. If you have won over the competition recently, determine why you were successful. If you've lost business to a competitor, find out why.

Analyze your customers. What are you offering that the competition isn't? In other words, what added value do you offer the customer, and would it be enough to ask for a better price?

Determine where you are different and better. Use this information to your advantage in presentations and proposals. Get testimonial letters. Showing letters of approval from customers helps prove that you are better than your competition. Include copies with proposals.

Create "win-win" deals. If customers want cheap solutions to short-term problems, help them focus on the long-term advantages of doing business with you. Ask to see proposals from price-cutting competitors. The customer may not realize what's not included.

Look for missing items such as training, sales and technical support, and other differentiating components. One word of caution, however. Customers are smarter than ever and they've heard it all before. Let them know that you are genuinely interested in helping them solve their problems.

Above all, don't become defensive. Be professional and polite in pointing out your strong points, but do so with enthusiasm. Always maintain your positive mental attitude. After all, even if a customer isn't buying today, don't give him a reason not to deal with you tomorrow.

Even if your product can be found at dozens of locations, great service will give a customer a reason to buy from you. Here's an example: Not long ago I went out to shop for a new car as visions of badly dressed, pushy salespeople and endless negotiating danced in my head. Often, by the time the whole miserable experience is over, you wish you'd just kept your old car. Not so this time. It was downright pleasant.

When I entered the dealership, the salesman introduced himself, gave me his card, and told me that he had been the top salesman at the dealership for years—which meant nothing to me. I couldn't have cared less. Then I saw a car that I really liked. He asked me if I wanted to drive it, and I said, "No, I'm not ready to buy yet. I'm just shopping."

He said, "No hurry. When you're ready, just let me know. I'll be happy to help if I can."

I made a mental note. I like this guy. A few weeks later, when I went back, I asked for him. I told him I was ready to buy a car and was interested in what kind of deal he could make. He asked for a minimal amount of information, arranged for the appraiser to look at the car I was trading in, and worked out the numbers. I agreed to the deal and he gave me a credit application to fill out and fax back to him at my convenience.

The next day he called to tell me the car was ready for me to pick up. He'd had it washed and filled it with gas. While I was signing the final papers, he transferred my stuff from my old car to my new one.

When I finished the paperwork, he took me to the car and showed me how to operate all the electronic gizmos on it, and he said, "I took the liberty of setting the radio buttons for you. My guess is you would like these stations," and he named them.

He'd sized me up pretty well. He was right on all but one station. I wonder if there's a connection between his service and the fact that he's been the top salesman for years. Guys like that are going to give car salesmen a good name.

—— POSITIVE ACTION STEPS ——

☞ Build a relationship first. Sales will come later.

☞ Don't try to "sell" prospects. Focus on solving their problems.

☞ Look for ways to add value to what you have to offer such as free training or support.

DAY 74

A MILLION-DOLLAR LESSON IN SELLING

We all know that no one can predict the future. We may not know the specifics, but we can control our destinies to a great extent. If we continually strive to succeed, we eventually will. If we give up and make excuses for our position in life, it will never get better.

One of the most valuable lessons I have learned about responsibility and my ability to control my future occurred as I sold life insurance to work my way through Southwestern Oklahoma State University. It was the perfect job for me. Just out of the Navy, I was a serious student with a family. I could attend classes in the morning, make sales calls in the afternoon and evening, and earn a decent living.

I had the good fortune to work for Glenn H. Wright, a former teacher and one of the best sales trainers I have ever known. When he recruited me, he was head of training for the corporate office, but he longed to return to his hometown of Weatherford. He opened a general agency there, and I worked for him. It was like having a personal trainer around the clock.

Glenn quickly taught me how to measure my effectiveness by keeping accurate records of all my activities. I soon learned that my sales volume was not left to chance—it was entirely within my control. Sales resulted from giving presentations. Opportunities to give presentations resulted from making calls. If I wanted to make more money, all I had to do was make more calls.

My effectiveness improved as I became more skilled, but the principles did not change. The most important lesson I learned from that experience was that some activities made money and some didn't. Filing and office work were important, but they were activities that could be done at any time. Only activities directly related to selling were profitable. I learned to do the profitable tasks as long as I had the opportunity each day, and to do the unprofitable tasks when it was too late in the day to call on customers.

I've carried that lesson with me for decades, and I've shared it with hundreds of others in my writings, seminars, and speeches. It is a lesson that has given me a competitive edge in everything I have ever attempted.

The second most valuable lesson was related to me by Wayne Bilut who said, "You'll make a lot more money by listening than you ever will by talking."

One of the nation's top printing salesmen, who for many years personally sold between eight and ten million dollars' worth of printing annually, today Bilut heads up Communilink, a Lake Forest, Illinois-based communications company. But he still spends most of his time in the field meeting clients, reviewing projects, and selling.

I first met Bilut almost twenty-five years ago. I had just graduated from college and landed a position with a company based in suburban Chicago. Bilut was making cold calls in my building, and he asked the receptionist if he could see the guy who bought printing for the company.

Having spent my college years working in sales, I wanted to meet a guy who had enough guts to go door to door in an office building making cold calls. I gave him a couple of printing jobs, and I soon found that Bilut was an exceptional person. He always delivered what he promised, on time and on budget, and his service was extraordinary. There were never any nasty surprises when he was on the case.

Over the years, sometimes I've done business with Bilut and sometimes not, depending on the situation, but he has always stayed in touch. Bilut is a quintessential salesperson. He loves selling and has been enormously successful at it.

His secret of success is simple. He merely provides quality products at a good value backed up by outstanding service. While those attributes are not at all hard to understand, they are incredibly difficult to put into practice.

Delivering on the promises of quality, value, and service that everyone talks about these days requires good management from the top of the organization to the bottom. It also requires listening, something that Bilut is very good at. He not only listens to what is being said, he also listens carefully to what has been omitted. He's made a lot of money over the years by figuring out what his clients worry about most, then making himself part of the solution.

You can do the same when you learn to really listen to what is being said—and not said.

POSITIVE ACTION STEPS

☞ Do profitable tasks as long as you have the time—you can attend to details later.

☞ Keep a record of your activities to find the most profitable times to perform each task.

☞ Listen at least as much as you talk.

DAY 75

SELL IT
WITH WRITING

Before you pack up the office and head out on the information superhighway, remember one thing: Whether it is contained in an old-fashioned letter or brochure, or in a high-tech e-mail message or fax, one of the best-selling tools you have is persuasive writing.

In today's lean and competitive world, you can significantly improve your effectiveness by adapting your face-to-face skills to written materials. Putting it in writing may provide you with an alternate channel for uncovering prospects, building accounts, and closing more and bigger deals.

Persuasive writing can help convey detail and is especially helpful in illustrating technical benefits to non-technical people. Written proposals also make it easier to present big-ticket items that will need management approval. The written word also can do a great job of selling the benefits of a new product or service.

You don't need fancy words or a gripping style. What you need to do is convey detailed information about how your product or service can fill a need for your customers and prospects, and you need to tell them in a persuasive manner.

Here are a few tips on making your written presentation more effective:

☞ Outline how you can help solve a prospect's problem or help them reach a goal.

☞ Clearly state a plan of action and where in the plan your product or service comes in.

☞ Guarantee your plan by showing how your plan cannot go wrong. Provide references of your other satisfied customers, and

☞ Give the prospect a call to action. Set a specific time when you will meet with them to discuss your proposal.

Just remember customers are interested in solving problems. They like to read about how important they are and what you can do for them, not how important you think your product is. You may be pleasantly surprised at your persuasiveness when you focus on your customer instead of yourself and your product.

Another way to sell it with writing is through the proper use of news releases. You can sometimes gain free publicity as well as a few customers by attracting the attention of the news media to your company's recent endeavors. If you have ever tried channeling your company's news to the local media, however, you may already know that the chances of seeing your release in print can be pretty slim.

As one editor friend said, "Remember you are writing to someone who opens the mail over a wastebasket." Find a new angle or twist with human interest to make your news item stand out from the stacks of releases editors receive daily.

The first step toward writing an effective news release is to avidly read the publications to which you submit material. Study the articles to determine what type of information editors will be looking for and the style in which copy is written.

As you write your news release, make sure you:

☞ Avoid technical jargon. Say what you have to say in clear, concise English.

☞ Be accurate. All claims must be valid.

☞ Keep proper tools within your reach (thesaurus, dictionary, grammar reference).

☞ Include photographs. Often a good feature photo with a clever caption will make it to publication when an article won't.

☞ Get acquainted with someone on the business beat of your local newspaper. Your release still has to have news value, but if the reporter or editor recognizes your name, your release has a better chance for survival. And you have a better shot at selling your products to new customers.

—— POSITIVE ACTION STEPS ——

☞ Gear your writing to how you can solve your client's problems—not how great your product is.

☞ Keep your proposals brief—just long enough to cover the subject and no longer.

☞ When you need to reach someone who isn't accepting calls, fax it.

☞ Use news releases to reach out to a wider audience.

DAY 76

KEEPING UP WITH WHAT'S UP

In these fast-paced times, it's easy for business executives and owners to become insulated from the day-to-day concerns of the business—even though it's often a fatal mistake to let this happen.

Some years ago, the company I worked for updated its facilities and included an employee cafeteria in our building. Old habits die hard, though, and many people continued to frequent a popular delicatessen nearby. In fact, the company president liked the special luncheon salads so much that he patronized the deli long after the company cafeteria opened.

Eventually, the friendliness of the staff, the convenience, and the quality of the food at the company cafeteria lured most employees away from the deli. At the deli, however, most of this activity went unnoticed. Based on past successes, the owners expanded, adding an ice cream parlor and a gift shop.

Gradually, the deli owners began to notice a drop in business. They ran in-store specials and reduced prices, but nothing seemed to help. They reasoned that it must be the recession, and that business would pick up with better times.

Today, that deli is out of business. The outcome could have been vastly different if the proprietors had been in closer touch with their customers and what was going on around them. A simple "I haven't seen you in here in a while" could have been enough to get a customer to tell them about the new cafeteria.

By staying in touch and learning about this new competition, they could have done a number of things. They could have initiated a delivery service to retain loyal customers during the cafeteria's uncertain early days. Even better, had they taken the time and trouble to find out that the company president was a satisfied customer, they might have been able to use that influence to get the catering contract for the cafeteria themselves.

They failed to use W. Clement Stone's R2A2 principle. They failed to recognize, relate, assimilate, and apply knowledge that was readily available to them.

It's easy for business executives to become insulated from day-to-day concerns of the business. It's also a mistake to let this happen. That's why Hyatt managers sometimes spend a day working as a hotel staffer, and why McDonald's executives cook burgers occasionally. It lets them know how hard their people are working, keeps them in touch with their customers, and reminds them just what business they are in.

John O'Toole writing in *Selling* magazine says, "Every sale, with the possible exception of those involving a vending machine, is a personal transaction. So success in selling depends, in no small measure, on the seller's ability to learn as much as possible about the prospect."

O'Toole says the best way to get close to a prospective customer is to learn something about his personal life as well as his business life. When you understand his or her personal goals, career plans, and personal philosophy, you can relate to him or her in just about any situation. It's not easy. The first step is to do your homework. Read your trade publications for articles by or about your potential customer, and check *Who's Who* or other biographies of important people in your industry. Ask your other customers or people in your organization who know your prospect about him. What's he like? Where's he from? Does he golf? Fish? Bowl?

If you are dealing with large numbers of consumers, O'Toole cautions, the job is going to be a whole lot tougher. Don't be seduced by demographic information that may seem wonderfully simple back at the home office, but is more distracting than helpful in the field.

For example, a demographic profile that reads, "white female, aged eighteen to forty-nine, urban, some college, household income $50,000-plus" sounds helpful until you realize that you are describing both Madonna and Tipper Gore. O'Toole says that any salesperson who would enter a "personal transaction" with Ms. Gore in the same manner and with the same sales strategy as he would use with Madonna had better have an independent source of income.

Market research may be compelling when it is presented in persuasive language supported by lots of nice tables and charts, but *Selling* says that if you only know your customers by demographic profile, you will never really know how to sell them. There is an old rule in selling that says people always have two reasons for not buying something: one that sounds good, and the real reason. You'll never know your prospects' real reasons unless you get to know them personally. It takes time, but it's worth the trouble.

—— POSITIVE ACTION STEPS ——

☞ Keep in touch with what's going on by talking to your employees, co-workers, and customers.

☞ Recognize, relate, assimilate, and apply the information that is readily available all around you.

☞ When conditions change, don't assume you know why. Ask your customers and workers.

DAY 77

BUSINESS AND PLEASURE

You've heard the maxim about not mixing business with pleasure. But talk to people who work for themselves, doing exactly what they want to do, and they'll tell you that work *can* be a pleasure.

Studies show that business owners often work fifty percent more hours than their employees. What those statistics don't say is that many of those owners work such long hours because they like it. The joy of working for yourself, where everything you do adds to your success, is a very powerful motivator.

All of this presupposes, of course, that you pick the right business for you. Many people go into a business because they think they will make a lot of money. There's nothing wrong with that, but if money is your only motivation, you will probably be miserable. You have to love what you're doing and be able to make a profit doing it.

Here are a few tips for those thinking about starting a business of your own. First, find the business you want to be in. Ask yourself, of all the jobs you've ever had, which ones did you really like doing and why?

Next, determine yourself if there really is a market for a business doing what you like to do. Turning a hobby into a business may seem like fun, but it won't be if there's no market for it.

If you want to open a business in a field you have no experience in, get a job in that field first. You can then learn the business from the inside while you decide, without risking any of your own money, whether you would really like to be in the business.

Ask yourself if you have all the skills needed to run this business, or will you need to find a partner with those skills you lack?

Finally, take a careful look at yourself and decide whether you have the discipline needed to get your business off the ground. Working for yourself can be fun and rewarding, but in the early, lean times, you may have to motivate yourself to keep going when you'd rather just give up.

Statistics show that on average we spend one-third of our lives at work. When you can find something you really love to do on your own terms, you are going to have a happier, more fulfilling life. You will also have a more successful one.

It's almost certainly going to take longer and be more difficult than you expect, as Jack Miller discovered. Born in Chicago in 1929, Miller got his first job at the age of eleven delivering dry cleaning on his bicycle, and he never stopped working.

He dug ditches, loaded freight cars, or "whatever hard, dirty job paid the most." He worked his way through college and at age twenty-seven decided it was time to begin his own business. He borrowed $2,000 from his father-in-law, set up an office in his bedroom at home, and used his uncle's basement as a warehouse.

He hit the streets at 6:30 a.m. and sold all day. The next morning, he'd call his orders in to the wholesaler, pick them up, separate them at home, take them to United Parcel Service for delivery, then go home, type up invoices, and mail them to customers.

Miller believes that success comes with no special genius. It results from plenty of hard work, good common sense, a desire to succeed, and a strong pursuit of excellence in every phase of the business.

At Quill Corporation, Miller's company, the commitment to excellence starts at the top. "You have to demand it of the other people in the organization," he says. "It has to be the standard. Whatever business you are in, you are in business for yourself. The product is you. We are each born with a certain amount of potential, and our whole life is a road to realizing a greater amount of potential."

Today, the company that began as an extra phone line is head-quartered on a 42-acre site in the Chicago suburb of Lincolnshire. Quill corporation employs more than 1,000 people and boasts sales in the hundreds of millions.

Part of that success is due to Quill's outstanding customer service. In 1970, long before it was fashionable, Quill adopted a Customer Bill of Rights.

Briefly it reads:

I. As a customer, you are entitled to be treated like a real, individual, feeling human being—with friendliness, honesty, and respect.

2. You are entitled to full value for your money.

3. You are entitled to a complete guarantee of satisfaction.

4. You are entitled to fast delivery.

5. You are entitled to speedy, courteous, knowledgeable answers on inquires.

6. You are entitled to be an individual dealing with other individuals.

7. You are entitled to be treated exactly as we want to be treated when we are someone else's customer.

Miller points out, "Most people don't know the value of a customer. It may be just a $100 sale today, but over a lifetime it may be $10,000 or more." Treating customers well pays big dividends.

—— POSITIVE ACTION STEPS ——

☞ Make excellence your standard. Remember the old saying, "If it's worth doing, it's worth doing well."

☞ Whatever business you are in, you are in business for yourself. The product is you.

☞ Decide for yourself: If you could have any job in the world, what would it be? Then go after it.

CHAPTER TWELVE

ENERGY AND ENTHUSIASM

Enthusiasm is the secret fuel that drives the success of most projects. If you're enthusiastic, others will be enthusiastic about you and what you wish to achieve. This chapter includes articles on enthusiasm and how to develop a personality that generates it.

DAY 78

ENTHUSIASM

Enthusiasm is the fuel that drives all accomplishment. Without it you will never be able to convince others that your ideas are worth pursuing. In fact, if you are not enthusiastic about your goals, you won't even be able to convince yourself to pursue them.

You have probably seen the power of enthusiasm in your friends and acquaintances. When they talk about something in which they really and truly believe, they take on an intensity you never see in any other part of their lives. They become more animated, they talk more forcefully, and they have an aura that is hard to resist. You soon find yourself beginning to feel persuaded to their point of view even though initially you may have disagreed with them. If you can develop enthusiasm, you can harness that type of energy to drive your success.

At work, enthusiasm makes your day much less difficult and monotonous. You will find your energy level is higher than it's ever been, and you don't seem to tire as easily. You will become a more dynamic person—the type that attracts others to you. It is simply impossible not to like an enthusiastic person.

The good news is that it is possible to learn to be enthusiastic. W. Clement Stone says that if you act enthusiastic, your emotions will follow, and soon enough you will be enthusiastic.

To act enthusiastic, Stone says to speak forcefully and with purpose. This is particularly helpful if you are upset or have "butterflies in your stomach" when you face an audience. Put emotion in your voice. Stress words that are important and hesitate where there would be a period or comma. Dramatic pauses draw listeners in. And keep a smile in your voice. Acting happy can go a long way toward eventually making you happy. Just remember it's not so much what you say as how you say it. Your tone and manner make a lasting impression on others.

Of course, you must believe in what you say. If you are not sincere and honest, others will soon begin to see through you.

You eventually will develop your own ways of inspiring enthusiasm within yourself, but a good place to start is to have a definite goal that you believe in with all your heart. Next you must believe in yourself, in your ability to accomplish any task you set before yourself. If you do, and if you act enthusiastically and concentrate on positive thoughts, honest, sincere enthusiasm will follow—and so will success.

Companies can also apply the principles of enthusiasm to help increase business, as the following story illustrates.

When Jack Reichert leafed through a Neiman-Marcus catalog, it suddenly occurred to him that the company he heads, Brunswick Corporation, shares the famous retailer's passion for quality. "I thought if there was anybody I knew who provided high-quality products, it's us; why don't we let the world know about it?"

That realization led to the introduction of a series of high-quality, limited-edition Brunswick products supported by an advertising campaign positioning the company as the maker of the best products of their kind.

The "Leadership Series," as Brunswick calls the campaign, had a very positive effect on its employees, according to the *Chicago Tribune*. "Morale in manufacturing operations has perked up as workers get a chance to put inlaid teakwood handles onto (gold plated Zebco) fishing rods or hand-build a billiard table with the same woods and glues used by Brunswick during the era when billiard tables were its only business."

That sort of pride and enthusiasm is exactly what managers need to demonstrate to their employees in order to lead them to higher levels of self-satisfaction and improved productivity, according to Arthur Levitt, Jr., chairman of the Securities Exchange Commission and former chairman of the American Business Conference.

In an address to the partners of the international accounting firm of KPMG Peat Marwick, Levitt reported the results of a study conducted by the American Business Conference, which showed that the basic ingredient of the success stories of the past decade is often a chief executive who is a "driven, committed, charismatic leader who understands the importance of quality." These people are able to project their values, their commitment, and their sense of excitement to an entire company. They can motivate employees to perform beyond the norm and to feel a sense of deep personal involvement with their work. Companies led by such people, Levitt said, have a passion for innovation and tend to compete on value rather than price.

Conversely, a company whose management appears to take little interest in the quality of its people and its products will find that attitude quickly spreading throughout the entire company. Further, once it is ingrained, it is extremely difficult to change a negative attitude into a positive one.

—— POSITIVE ACTION STEPS ——

☞ To be enthusiastic, act enthusiastic.

☞ Make an effort to act enthusiastic about your work.
Post a reminder to be enthusiastic in your work area.

☞ Associate with positive, enthusiastic
people. Enthusiasm is contagious.

DAY 79

LEARNING FROM DEFEAT

If you've ever been tempted to make excuses for your failures instead of owning up to them and taking the necessary action to prepare yourself for success, you might be interested in the story of Tom Dempsey.

Dempsey was born without half of a right foot and only a stub of a right arm. But like most other boys, he wanted to play sports. More than anything else, he wanted to play football.

Because he had such a burning desire to play the game, his parents had a prosthetic foot made for him. It was carved out of wood and encased in a special football shoe. Hour after hour, day after day, Tom Dempsey practiced kicking the football with his wooden foot. He would try and try again to make field goals, each time moving further and further from the goal posts. He eventually became so proficient that he was recruited by the New Orleans Saints.

On November 8, 1970, Tom Dempsey got his big chance. The Saints were trailing the Detroit Lions by a single point with two seconds remaining in the game. No doubt some of the fans and perhaps even the players thought it was crazy when the Saints teed up the football for a field goal attempt—from sixty-three yards out. The roar of the crowd could be heard all over the country when the ball tumbled through the air, end over end, and sailed between the uprights.

On that crisp November day, Tom Dempsey set the world record for the longest field goal—a record that was not broken for 43 years.

The Detroit Lions' coach Joseph Schmidt said, "We were beaten by a miracle."

It was a miracle—a miracle of the determination and persistence of a young man who refused to accept as a handicap the physical limitation with which he was born. He overcame the adversity and went on to perform a feat that the world's finest athletes were unable to duplicate.

Tom Dempsey's amazing feat stands as a beacon of hope and inspiration to every one of us who has tried and failed, and tried and failed again. We know that if we persevere, we will eventually prevail.

In fact, researchers recently discovered that attitude is one of the most important factors in achieving success in life. For a few days, the results of a survey about the importance of attitude were a hot topic of discussion on the talk show circuit. What was surprising was that apparently this fact was news to a lot of people.

It is a stone fact that if you think you will fail, you already have failed. On the other hand, if you believe you are going to be successful, you will succeed. You may not succeed on the first try, but you will eventually prevail. You will almost certainly have setbacks, and there will be times when it seems that you have failed miserably.

Everybody does. Virtually every person who achieves great things in life fails, sometimes spectacularly. What separates them from the losers is that they simply don't accept defeat as permanent. They recognize that there are always external forces that are beyond their control.

You cannot control circumstances, but you can control your attitude toward them. Regardless of how many setbacks you encounter, if you examine them carefully, you will find that they aren't setbacks at all. They are learning opportunities. If you approach them positively and learn from your mistakes, you cannot fail for long. It's an idea that is so simple anyone can understand it, yet it is incredibly difficult to put into practice.

Positive thinking is not something that most of us do automatically. It's something that must be learned. You become a positive person by training yourself to replace negative thoughts with their positive counterpart the moment that they first appear. And you keep doing it until it becomes an automatic reaction to replace "I can't" with "I will!"

When people ask me if positive thinking really works, I tell them, and I'll tell you, that I'll bet you can't think of a single situation in which it would be better to think negatively than to think positively. There simply isn't one. Whatever you hope to accomplish, you can accomplish if you truly believe you can.

—— POSITIVE ACTION STEPS ——

☞ Defeat is temporary if your commitment is permanent.

☞ When faced with adversity, remember those who have overcome even greater obstacles and succeeded.

☞ When you fail, try again. If you fail again, try again.

DAY 80

SEARCHING FOR HIGHER MOUNTAINS

It is a characteristic of goal setting that when we reach one goal, we almost automatically begin to reach for even greater heights. Because most achievers are working toward several goals simultaneously, often, by the time you achieve a short- or intermediate-term goal, you are already thinking about the next mountain to climb.

The more we progress, the more we need to expand our goals to keep us challenged, to make sure we are always moving forward.

For most of us, success is a cumulative process. We form the habit of becoming winners by winning a little every day, by working hard to achieve our goals.

Winners take risks, but they are managed risks. They evaluate their options carefully and invest their time and money in opportunities that offer the most promise. They know that if they follow the tried and true principles, success will eventually come.

This does not in any way mean you should think small. Far from it. Your thoughts should be grand, but your plan for achieving your goals should be precise, methodical, and broken down into small, manageable pieces. Never allow yourself or anyone else to erect barriers to your achievement.

Just as the mind has a habit of seeking new and higher goals, it also has a habit of respecting boundaries. If you believe something is impossible or that you can only achieve a certain level of success, that will become your reality.

Someone once told me a great story about an experiment that was conducted with two fish. The fish were different species, and one normally fed on the other. Researchers constructed a special aquarium with a glass divider in the center that created an invisible barrier between the two types of fish.

When they were first placed in the aquarium, the predator fish repeatedly banged against the glass in a futile attempt to reach the other. As time passed, however, he accepted the existence of the barrier and eventually gave up. Some time later, a researcher removed the divider, but each fish continued to swim benignly in his respective zone, unaware that the barrier no longer existed.

One of the greatest barriers you may encounter is fear of success. Joan C. Harvey, a Ph.D. in the University of Pennsylvania Medical School's psychiatry department, identifies six types of people who exhibit a fear of success.

Workaholics. These people, Harvey says, "attribute their achievements solely to extraordinary efforts." They always prepare longer, more thoroughly, and more compulsively for exams, presentations, or projects than do their peers. Every test, every report, every meeting is critical because they believe that each of these things has the potential to expose them as frauds.

Any praise or recognition offers little enjoyment to workaholics; they are already beginning preparation for the next project. They see all successes as the result of hard work because hard work never varies. It's a never-ending struggle to defeat their self-perceived stupidity, mediocrity, or inadequacy.

Magical thinkers. Akin to workaholics, magical thinkers have refined over-preparation to an art form, motivating themselves by almost ritualistically calling up visions of failure. Because they succeed, they associate success with worry, and frequently believe that if they ever allow themselves to optimistically anticipate success, fate will punish them with failure.

Charmers. These types—usually women, but sometimes men—are attractive, likable people who flatter, entertain, or flirt with their superiors and mentors. Because they use their good looks, personality, and wit to create a good impression, they find themselves in a confusing, ambiguous situation when they achieve success. Self-doubt convinces them that their appearance and social skills have blinded their superiors to the inadequacies they think they have.

Harvey says that charmers believe their personal attractiveness creates "a sort of halo effect" that clouds the judgment of experts. Any praise or reward they receive is immediately devalued as a mistake.

Mimics. These characters believe that, in order to be accepted, they must suppress their own opinions and promote the view of those whose approval they seek. They never publicly disagree with their bosses or mentors, and they will often publicly support ideas with which they secretly find fault, thus furthering their own belief that they are impostors.

Chameleons. Similar to mimics, but more sophisticated, chameleons not only imitate, they behave in a complementary fashion. They intuitively know both the obvious and subtle needs of a mentor or superior, and are multidimensional enough to fill those needs. They seek approval by responding with appropriate behavior, whether it is in the form of a challenge, with sympathy, or with sex. Yet when they do receive the desired validation of their ability, talent, or intelligence, they can't accept it because they see it as a result of their own manipulations rather than as something that is truly deserved.

Shrinking violets. These people are extremely modest and very reluctant to accept compliments. They deflect praise with a demure, "Thank you, but…" and proceed to point out minor deficiencies in their work or to discuss at length how it could have been improved. They profoundly fear being thought of as arrogant; they feel that a display of pride on their part will result in punishment—in the form of either a humiliating failure or in being exposed as an impostor of low or mediocre ability. Shrinking violets are impelled to deny compliments because they believe acknowledging and accepting praise will only hasten their eventual downfall.

As you grow and develop and reach higher and higher goals, you will find that some of the barriers that limited you in the past have disappeared, along with your fear of success. But you will never know this truth unless you continue to challenge those barriers.

—— POSITIVE ACTION STEPS ——

☞ Stretch yourself. When you reach one
goal, choose another higher one.

☞ Continually challenge the barriers to your success.
One day you may find they have crumbled.

☞ Never give up on your goal.

DAY 81

PLEASING PERSONALITY II

Ask the first dozen people you meet what personality is, and you'll get a dozen different answers. Most will agree, however, that your personality is a big factor in determining your success or failure in life. There are a number of things you can do to develop a pleasing personality.

Napoleon Hill said that personality cannot be defined in one word. It is the sum of those qualities which distinguish you from every other person on earth. The clothes you wear form a part of your personality, but not all of it. Your facial expression forms part of your personality, but it not your whole personality either. The words you speak form the numerous lights and shades which blend into one another and constitute your personality. Your voice constitutes one of these lights and shades. Also the manner in which you shake hands forms a part of your personality.

An attractive personality may be described generally as one that draws people to you and causes them to find companionship in your company, while an unattractive personality causes people to want to get as far away from you as possible.

An attractive, magnetic personality usually can be found in the person who speaks gently and kindly, selecting words that do not offend; someone who selects clothing of appropriate style, varying in colors that properly harmonize; who is unselfish and willing to serve others; who is a friend of all humanity, regardless of wealth or creed, nationality or color; someone who refrains from speaking unkindly of those who are not present.

A pleasant personality can also be found in the person who manages to converse without being drawn into argument or trying to draw others into argument or idle gossip; who sees the good there is in people and overlooks the bad; someone who seeks neither to reform or reprimand others; who smiles frequently; someone who loves children, flowers, birds, the growing grass, the trees, the running brooks, and the open air; someone who sympathizes with those who are in trouble; who forgives acts of unkindness; who willingly grants to others the right to believe as they choose regarding politics and religion; who earnestly strives to be constructive in every thought and action; someone who encourages others and spurs them on to greater effort in some useful work for humanity.

It is possible, of course, to change your habits—and your personality—to become the person you wish to be. It doesn't automatically follow, of course, that because you change, others will notice. You can, however, alter people's perception of you through the use of a principle the advertising community calls positioning.

Here's how it works: Because the mind is selective in what it will and will not accept, we develop a hierarchy of information. New ideas are related to what we already know and placed in their proper position in the hierarchy. Advertisers attempt to establish a niche in consumers' minds by relating their products to what we already know.

The best example of the concept of positioning is the classic Avis-vs.-Hertz campaign: "We're No. 2; we try harder." Sales soared, not because Avis tried harder, but because we identified with the company's claim that it tried harder to please its customers.

You can use the principle to your advantage in any profession or in any line of business. If you want your customers to perceive you as a person who cares about quality, for example, you must project quality not only in your advertising, but in every aspect of the way you do business. If you want your employer to perceive you as a reliable, responsible executive, you must behave responsibly in every situation.

The image you project should be built on your particular strengths and based on truth (a lie is quickly spotted). It should be managed with the same care that you develop positive, successful habits to replace those that you wish to change or discard. Think about how you would like others to perceive you, then make sure your actions support your goal. Your correspondence, your conversations—all your dealings with others—should take into consideration how others will react to you.

—— POSITIVE ACTION STEPS ——

☞ Smile.

☞ Never speak ill of anyone.

☞ Take a genuine interest in those around you.

DAY 82

GOOD JUDGMENT

Someone once said that good judgment comes from experience. And where does experience come from? Bad judgment.

Many years ago, I worked with an exceptional professional photographer named Roy Watson. Roy not only did good work, he often did it while he was flying his own plane. As a passenger on some of those trips, I can tell you that it was a little unnerving when Roy stood the plane on its wing so he could lean out the window to take an aerial photo, but he always got some great shots.

Aside from the adventure of it all, the reason I most liked working with Roy was that he always encouraged me to bring along my own camera to take some pictures myself. I thought this was pretty odd for a guy who made his living taking pictures, so I asked him why he was so accommodating to an amateur photographer.

He replied with a question of his own. "Do you know the difference between a professional and an amateur?" he asked. When I told him that I didn't, he said, "An amateur is making his mistakes for the first time."

I've thought about his definition a lot since, and I don't know that even after all these years I would be able to come up with a better one. In the strictest sense, being a professional simply means that you charge for your services. In a broader sense, we expect a true professional to have a body of knowledge and a set of skills that he or she can quickly bring to bear to give us sound advice or to help us develop a solution to a problem. But I would suggest to you that the most reliable professionals, those we would most like to have at the controls of the 747 we're riding in or sitting beside us when we're called in for an IRS audit, are those who've been tempered by some practical experience in addition to all the theoretical knowledge they've accumulated over the years.

There's a great story about an executive who made a decision that cost the company ten million dollars. He quite naturally assumed that he would be fired for such a costly mistake, so he decided to take the offensive. He went to see his boss and said, "You don't have to fire me. I'll resign."

"Fire you!" his boss exclaimed. "Are you kidding? We just spent ten million dollars educating you. We're not about to fire you." Don't you wish you had a boss like that? Better still, don't you wish you were a boss like that?

You can be if you give your employees the room to grow and make mistakes with the proper motivation. But be careful. "An employee can be motivated without being productive, or without being satisfied," states *Executive Productivity* newsletter. And this kind of ineffective motivation, resulting in "a herd of poorly managed but highly motivated people would be a frightening sight."

To ensure performance improvement, motivation must be properly directed. Here are four suggestions, which *Executive Productivity* credits to researchers at the University of Cincinnati and Rensselaer Polytechnic Institute:

1. Treat all your subordinates with dignity and respect, and reassure them that they will not be left alone if they take risks and fail.

2. Since motivation is mostly emotional, toss aside the intellectual analyzing. If something works, don't ask why. Just leave it alone and hope it spreads.

3. Make changes in your employees' routine, even if it merely means switching them from one dull job to another. "For instance," say the researchers, "a checker in a supermarket who's done nothing but push buttons and make change will find a switch refreshing, even if it's only an afternoon in the produce department, bagging celery."

4. Reward success quickly. With many formal recognition systems, too much time elapses between success and reward, so supplement your formal system with an informal one that is faster.

—— POSITIVE ACTION STEPS ——

☞ Mistakes build experience. Minimize them, but don't fear them.

☞ Give others room to fail occasionally—it builds character, strength, and experience.

☞ The only mistake that is tragic is the one that is repeated. Learn from your mistakes.

DAY 83

ENTHUSIASM: CATCH IT

If you have ever worried about how today's kids will turn out, you're not alone. Anyone can tell you that kids today are dumber, lazier, and more violent than ever before. Or are they?

Not long ago, I was invited by a teacher I know to guest lecture to four classes of seventh graders. It's been several decades since I was a seventh grader, and I wasn't at all sure I could relate to them even though I have had a couple of seventh graders of my own. I know it's hard to hold their attention at that age. Maybe because I was flattered, or perhaps because I couldn't resist the challenge, I agreed.

When the appointed day arrived, I went to the school with more than a little apprehension. I shouldn't have worried. I thoroughly enjoyed myself, and I learned a couple of valuable lessons in the process.

I've been as critical as anyone of the public school system in this country, but very quickly I realized it isn't easy to deliver the same lecture over and over again with the enthusiasm and conviction that each group deserves. But the most profound lesson came at the end of the day.

My hostess warned me that the last class of the day would be the most difficult. They were a bunch of underachievers and rowdies, she said. They may have been underachievers, but they sure weren't dumb. They quickly grasped the concepts, they asked questions, they joked with me; in short, they were great fun. If being a rowdy means joking and making learning fun, I'm all for it. Learning is fun. It's too bad you have to graduate high school to realize what a joy learning can be.

As I reflected on the day, I realized that the last group—the underachievers and the rowdies—would probably achieve far more in their lives than the studious ones who meekly follow all the teacher's instructions. The personality traits that make them unsuccessful in school—things like creativity, personality, enthusiasm, and a sense of humor—are exactly the things that will make them successful later in life.

Einstein was a terrible student, Thomas Edison's teacher thought he was slow, and Barbara Streisand was a misfit, a shy, introverted girl with no friends. It may well be that a kid you're worried about today will grow up to be the next Einstein or Edison or Streisand.

That's not to say that discipline isn't necessary. Discipline is the force that channels enthusiasm into positive, constructive pursuits. Without it, we would never accomplish anything worthwhile in life. In fact, without discipline, the entire fabric of our society would unravel.

Not long ago, I found myself in a very strange position. Like most teenagers, my twin daughters Amy and Betsy watch too much television. Of course, the programs they like best are not historical documentaries or "The Three Tenors" in concert. They like sitcoms with weird characters who scream at each other or kids who make fools of adults.

We require them to earn the right to watch television, and we limit the number of hours they are allowed to watch, but like typical teenagers, they seem to conveniently forget the rules when it's time to turn off the TV. It's always a hassle.

Finally, one day I was so tired of their arguing about television that I said, "Look, I'm tired of fighting with you two about turning off the TV. If you want to turn your brains to mush watching these stupid programs, I don't care. Watch it all day. Watch it every day. Watch it twenty-four hours a day."

In a few minutes, something happened that was nothing short of miraculous. They turned off the TV and said, "We were thinking maybe we would help clean the kitchen. We're tired of that program anyway."

Even more amazing, they did it. And they did a good job.

Afterward, we had a long talk, and the gist of it was that they knew they needed discipline, and they appreciated our setting boundaries for them. They didn't at all like me telling them that I didn't care about them wasting their time. That meant I didn't care about them.

I promised them that I would never again do anything to make them believe that I didn't care about them, and they promised they would try to be more responsible about disciplining themselves. So now, when they complain about having to turn off the TV, I warn them that if they keep it up, I may have to become lenient again. And they say, "No, Dad. Anything but that!"

I may be the only parent on the planet who gets a positive response by threatening to be more permissive. It won't last forever, of course, but I intend to enjoy it while it does.

If only we could all find ways to set guidelines without destroying our kids' natural enthusiasm, what a lively, entertaining, and fulfilling world this would be.

—— POSITIVE ACTION STEPS ——

☞ Try to capture the natural enthusiasm of
kids who thrive on new challenges.

☞ Do not blindly follow the status quo. Questioning
the routine often leads to unique solutions.

☞ Stay enthusiastic on the job by learning a new skill or
learning about the organization and your place in it.

DAY 84

DEFEAT IS TEMPORARY

Napoleon Hill, once noted, "There is a vast difference between failure and temporary defeat."

Napoleon Hill's grandfather was a farmer and wagon builder in North Carolina during the late 1800s. When he cleared the land for farming, he always left an occasional oak tree alone in the fields, at the mercy of the elements. He knew that away from the shelter of the forest, those solitary trees would develop the strength to withstand Nature's greatest fury. And it was from those trees that the old craftsman made the wagon's wheels. The wood from those mighty oaks was strong and tough, hardy enough to support the wagon's load as it traveled across the land.

That experience led young Hill to speculate that like those powerful oak trees, we grow strong only when we are tested. We all face temporary obstacles. Seldom does anything go precisely according to plan. But it's because of the obstacles that get in our way that we gain the strength to deal with the difficulties we all face in our everyday lives. Adversity makes us stronger and prepares us for the time when we will eventually succeed. And if you persevere, you will eventually succeed.

There's a reason why a lot of people who were born poor grew up to be enormously successful. They learned to work hard, they learned to work smart, and they learned to persevere. They knew that if they had a problem, they had to figure out how to solve it. No one else would do it for them.

If you examine the lives of really successful people, you will find that they have discovered a great secret that you can use to your advantage. The secret of their success is this: They have discovered that temporary defeat is nothing more than that—it is temporary. It is really a great learning opportunity.

There will always be setbacks. They are part of life, but it is from our mistakes that we learn the most valuable lessons, lessons that we will never forget, lessons that will prepare us for success. There will always be problems, but within those problems are opportunities. That problems occur is not really important. How you deal with them is what matters. If you recognize the seed of an equal or greater opportunity in every adversity, as Napoleon Hill advised, and you recognize that adversity only moves you a step closer to achieving your goals, no one on earth can stop you.

In inventor Fred Allgood's view, creativity is a close cousin to problem solving. "The best thing anyone can ever do for me is to present me with a problem," he says.

The president and CEO of Fort Worth, Texas-based Allgood Products, Inc., Allgood holds twenty-five patents, mostly in the medical field. He wasn't born a genius. In fact, he told me as a kid he had lots of problems. He was a slow reader, he had a speech impediment, and he thought he was hopelessly dumb. So did the teachers who placed him in a class for slower students.

He got a lucky break when one teacher took an interest in him and helped him recognize—and correct—his problems. He began to do better in school, and when he graduated from high school he got a job working in a hospital as a surgical assistant. He quickly became popular with the surgeons because he had a knack for gadgetry. He was constantly tinkering with the surgical instruments and making them better.

He is now on a retainer from a surgical products manufacturer to develop more new products. Allgood doesn't see his ability as a particularly special gift. He says any time you see a problem, it is really an opportunity for an invention. When you hear someone complaining about how "this thing never works right," you have just discovered an opportunity to invent something that works better.

Here's what he suggests to capitalize on your ideas:

1. Write down your idea so you won't forget it.

2. Test every idea no matter how crazy it seems at first. Keep trying until you find one that works.

3. Don't show your idea to your friends too soon. They may try to talk you out of it because they don't understand it.

4. A lot of people may try to discourage you, but companies are always looking for new ideas. Find the one that's right for your idea.

5. You will have problems. The reasons something won't work will always show themselves. You won't have to look for them. Instead, concentrate on ways to make your idea work.

POSITIVE ACTION STEPS

☞ Realize defeat is temporary—unless you develop a "defeatist" attitude.

☞ Defeat brings with it opportunity—look for it.

☞ Never give up.

CHAPTER THIRTEEN

A FEW MORE WHO DARED

This chapter contains articles that chronicle the difficulties others have overcome to achieve great success.

THE DOMINO EFFECT: TOM MONAGHAN

How does a humble pizza maker become the president of one of the biggest pizza corporations in the world? According to Tom Monaghan, founder of Domino's Pizza and former Detroit Tigers' owner, he did it by setting definite goals for himself.

"Writing is the key to my system of goal setting," says Monaghan. He carries around a legal pad at all times to write down his plans, dreams, even possible problems and their solutions. Practically every thought that comes into his mind, Monaghan says he writes down on his pad. When one pad is full, he starts another.

"Over the last twenty years, I have accumulated dozens of packing boxes full of these pads. But the funny thing is I never look at them again once I'm finished writing," says Monaghan. He believes that simply writing things down is the important part of the process for him. Once he has written them out they are firmly planted in his mind.

In his autobiography, *Pizza Tiger*, Monaghan says, "I set long-range goals, annual goals, monthly, weekly, and daily goals. The long-range goals are dream sheets. But other lists are definite and action-oriented and specific.

"My goal list for one year, for example," says Monaghan, "began with this entry, '500 Units,' which meant that we would have a total of 500 units by the end of that year. A tough goal to meet. The important thing about this goal, though, is that it was specific. It wasn't just 'let's increase the number of units this year.' It was 500 or bust!"

Monaghan points out, "If a goal is specific, it is easier to communicate to others. This is important because when you are dealing with a corporate goal you have to sell it to the people who can help you achieve it." He says that before they can act on your goal, they have to first understand it, and then they must believe that it can be done and that they are capable of making it happen.

Monaghan also believes that in order to be effective, goals should have strict time limits. For instance, make your goal to achieve something this month or this year, not just sometime or when you get to it.

Monaghan also believes in "going public" with your goals. He learned this when he tried to quit smoking back in 1952. "I told everyone I knew that 'This is it. I have smoked my last cigarette.' That gave me the strength to follow through. If you believe you're going to do something, and tell everybody else you're going to do it, their belief will be a backstop for yours."

Monaghan also points out another reason for his success is his unshakable faith in a greater power. "I know I would not have been able to build Domino's without the strength I gained from my religious faith." In the early years, racked by a series of major setbacks, Monaghan says it was his faith that always saw him through.

Today Monaghan puts his religious beliefs to work by telling his employees and franchisees that "all they have to do to be successful is to have a good product, give good service, and apply the Golden Rule."

By having his employees and franchisees treat the customer as they would want to be treated, he has been able to build a giant empire on a simple product—pizza.

Domino's has had some problems lately. But like every other business, it had to weather the bad times and capitalize on the good. I would bet that Tom Monaghan has a yellow pad somewhere with a strategy mapped out for staying on top in the pizza wars.

—— POSITIVE ACTION STEPS ——

☞ Write down your goals to help
crystallize them in your mind.

☞ Be specific in your goals. Vague
goals bring vague results.

☞ Make your goals tough. A goal that takes
little work is generally worth little itself.

DAY 86

SWEET SONG OF SUCCESS: MICHELE BLOOD

Australian singer and songwriter Michele Blood read motivational and inspirational books in a hospital bed as she recovered from a near-fatal automobile accident. It was the beginning of a process that would forever change the course of her life.

Blood's injuries were so severe that doctors told her that while she might recover, she would have permanent physical limitations for the remainder of her life. It was a prognosis she refused to accept. She decided to defy the experts and take charge of her own healing process.

She read voraciously, studying books with positive, life-affirming messages, and listened to motivational tapes. As she listened, she realized that although she had listened to the tapes before, she had never actually written down what she heard.

Gradually, an idea began to take shape. She could combine the messages of healing with her musical skills and write her own affirmation songs. She credits the perfect health she enjoys today to the power of those positive musical affirmations.

Since the accident, Blood says she sees every challenge as an opportunity to "learn more, to grow more as a person, and to absolutely not care what other people think of me. I have learned to listen to my own inner voice. My love for God and my love for myself keeps me going because I know in my heart that everything is good, that nothing is wrong." She is so convinced of the power of such love that she named her company L.O.V.E. Management, an acronym for Love Of Vast Experience.

When obstacles arise, Blood recalls a Napoleon Hill anecdote: "'Show me a person with big success,' Napoleon Hill once said, 'and I'll show you a person with big problems.' Once when he was giving a speech, someone approached him and told of the many problems he had and asked Dr. Hill how he could get rid of them. And Napoleon Hill said, 'I can show you some people who have no problems.' He then walked with the individual about two blocks to the local cemetery. Pointing to the headstones, he said, 'There are thousands of people with no problems.'

"So you don't look at them as problems. You view them as challenges. And you will have challenges. Welcome them. The bigger the challenges, the more successful you can visualize yourself as becoming. Those challenges help you to grow. With every challenge, you break down more barriers and more fears."

Blood believes that anyone can become "a magnet to success, to riches in all forms. With positive thought backed by true feeling," she says, "you can and will begin to achieve everything you desire. Nothing is impossible.

"All you need is an idea, deep desire, and persistence," Blood advises. "Never, ever give up on your dreams. Don't compromise your master plan. Refuse all offers of compromise. Because of the nature of compromise, once you have compromised, you will have to keep on compromising. You will never truly achieve your dreams."

Make your plans, she suggests, but don't divulge them to anyone else. You don't need anyone else's approval, and you don't need to convince anyone. Their doubts can cause you to lose faith in yourself and your dream. Just keep believing, knowing that the same mind that gave you your dreams will also lead you to the right people and open the doors of opportunity. It just takes time. At the right time and the right place, your success will become manifest.

Blood is a great advocate of action. "I don't remember where I heard this or if I read it somewhere, but to me it sums it up beautifully," she says. "Tell everyone in the world what you are going to do, but first show them. Do everything that is necessary to help you achieve your goals. Spend a part of every day on personal development: visualizing, thinking, feeling, affirming, reading, and studying. This helps you clarify your goals—something that is vitally important—because it leads to power."

The ever-positive Blood believes that there are three essential components of success: knowledge, skills, and attitude. Most people think knowledge and skills are most important, she says, but studies have shown that knowledge and skills only contribute about 15 percent of the total makeup of people. "The major component is attitude, attitude, attitude," she says.

Affirmations are a wonderful way to develop a positive attitude and climb the ladder of success, Blood says emphatically: "Sing them, speak them, write them down, become them. Never underestimate the power of the spoken word. Take action on your ideas, and always give thanks to your Higher Power, knowing that what you really desire has already become a reality."

Blood recommends emotionalizing affirmations through song. ("I am a magnet to money. Money loves me.") She believes that go-getters are goal setters. Write down your goals—not just money goals. Fun goals. Outrageous goals. This will fill you with magnetic power. When you convince yourself, results will follow.

—— POSITIVE ACTION STEPS ——

☞ Use affirmations to keep your mind positive.
Write them, say them aloud, and sing them.

☞ Welcome problems. View them as opportunities
to grow and achieve bigger goals.

☞ Positive thought backed by true feeling will
allow you to achieve anything you desire.

DAY 87

SUCCESS SECRETS OF RICHARD BRANSON

A self-styled "adventure capitalist" who has crossed the Atlantic ocean twice in a speedboat and both the Atlantic and the Pacific in a hot air balloon, Richard Branson is a man whose chief requirements in life are met, according to *Vanity Fair* magazine, "whenever a great force of will can be set against singularly bad odds."

Branson has made a fortune doing what others thought couldn't be done, and his exploits of derring-do have become legend. He's water-skied behind a blimp, he's parachuted from airplanes, and he was delivered to his own wedding dangling from the landing struts of a helicopter.

Britain's premier entrepreneur demonstrated his knack for capitalizing on his business sense, wit, and keen sense of humor at age eighteen. His first venture was the launch of *Student* magazine in 1968. The upstart magazine garnered a good deal of publicity for Branson, largely because of his ability to persuade British celebrities to write for him.

Despite its high-profile launch, the magazine did not do well, but it did lead Branson into the record business. Accounts of the launch of Virgin Records differ, but as a result of one very successful advertisement, *Student* went into the mail-order record business.

The record business prospered and evolved into a recording studio and the Virgin Records label. Virgin Records has since grown into one of the top six record companies in the world, and it was the cash Virgin Records generated that enabled Branson to start Virgin Atlantic.

"I don't like taking risks," he says. "That sounds contradictory to the balloon thing, but I think that I'm protected against most of the downsides before going into something.

"I think one has to accept that everything is probably not going to be great. An entrepreneur will take calculated risks and not everything he does will be successful. He is going to have to push himself and his people and his company forward. You put a toe in the water to see how it feels before you jump in," he says.

The "balloon thing" to which Branson referred is his penchant for daredevil adventures like crossing the Atlantic ocean that have made him an international celebrity and almost killed him twice.

"There is obviously a risk that you may not come home from the adventure, but if you do, the satisfaction of having achieved it is very great. If we worry too much about the risk and not enough about the possibilities, a lot of things would never have happened," he said.

Branson's hijinks often mask his serious business side. He believes business should be fun, but it must be about building a worthwhile enterprise, creating jobs, and making money.

"I think most companies and most people forget that having a good time is very important. When companies forget it, people won't enjoy life. I would like to live so that when I reach the age of eighty or ninety, I can look back and feel quite pleased and happy with the life I've lived," Branson said.

Richard Branson's success formula made him a billionaire when he was barely into his forties. He offers this advice for capitalizing on opportunity:

1. Learn from your mistakes and correct them.

2. Don't avoid risk. Minimize it. Protect yourself against the downside while positioning yourself to take advantage of the upside.

3. When you are faced with a difficult decision, take time to clear your mind and give yourself time to think through the options.

4. Don't think too much about the risk and not enough about the possibilities. Unless we are willing to push ourselves, nothing goes forward.

—— POSITIVE ACTION STEPS ——

☞ Each day, push yourself to be just a little better. Push another step closer to your ultimate goal.

☞ Take a chance. Minimize the risks, but every once in a while take a chance on bettering yourself.

☞ Have fun. If working toward your goal isn't fun for you, perhaps you have chosen the wrong goal.

DAY 88

DICK DEVOS LEADING THE WAY AT AMWAY

Growing up the child of a successful parent is a mixed blessing," according to Dick DeVos, president of Amway Corporation, one of the world's largest direct-selling companies. "There's no way to replace the kinds of experiences and instruction that I have been able to experience. There is also no question that I have had to live up to some high expectations."

The son of Amway co-founder Richard DeVos, Dick DeVos spent fifteen years with his father's company before leaving in 1989 to launch his own investment firm. He returned to Amway in late 1992 when his father retired following a heart attack.

DeVos, who also serves as president of The Orlando Magic professional basketball team, which the family owns, said there is an important distinction between his situation and many other second generation managers of family businesses. "Sometimes the younger generation is not encouraged to live outside the shadow of their parents to gain confidence in themselves and their own abilities and talents.

"My parents never forced us into anything. They told us: 'We want you to be the best you can be with whatever God has given you. Go do that, and you'll be happier and we'll be happier.' That removed the cloud for us. They encouraged us to be ourselves, and they never tried to take credit for our accomplishments."

DeVos had, in fact, already made his mark on the company his father founded in 1959 with Jay Van Andel to sell a cleaning product out of their basements. Joining Amway in 1974, Dick DeVos worked in a variety of positions in research and development, manufacturing and distribution, marketing, sales, finance, public relations, and government affairs. In 1984, he was named vice president international with responsibility for Amway affiliate operations in 18 countries. Under his leadership, sales more than tripled, and international sales exceeded domestic sales for the first time in the company's history.

Headquartered in Ada, Michigan (a suburb of Grand Rapids), in 1994 Amway posted sales of $3.9 billion, and international sales accounted for two-thirds of the company's revenues.

A quietly confident leader, DeVos doesn't plan to make radical changes. "We have a great responsibility to our 10,000 employees and over two million distributors," he said. There are a lot of people who are directly linked to this company, and their families rely on our making good decisions and keeping our promises."

Treating every person as an individual is a key responsibility of a leader, and an important component in Amway's success, DeVos believes. "There is a view that is prevalent in politics and some businesses that individuals are merely pieces of a group, and that individuals are subordinate to the group," he said.

"At Amway, individuals are superior to the group. We try to treat every employee as an individual and recognize each one for the contribution he or she makes. I don't care what part of the machine they are. Every machine needs each of its parts to run.

"We make every effort to align their personal interests with the best interests of our organization so that when they are working with us, they are achieving two goals. They are improving their life and the company," he said.

Amway recognizes outstanding performers through a variety of incentives and awards, and encourages employees and distributors to read positive publications and listen to motivational tapes. "Creating a positive environment is absolutely, fundamentally critical to success," DeVos said. "We are all influenced by the environment around us.

"My father gave a speech once that I liked very much. He talked about the three As of success—action, attitude, and atmosphere. People often focus on action, but if you don't get the attitude and atmosphere right, how do you think you're going to get the kind of action you would like?

"When you are around people who encourage you and support and challenge you to be better than you think you can be, the result is creation of an atmosphere that results in a positive attitude that when combined with hard work is much more likely to translate into appropriate action." Amway also strives to motivate people by giving them more flexibility than they might find elsewhere. "Individuals' lives today are fast-paced, and there are a lot of changes," DeVos said. "In the old days people would go to work at eight o'clock and come home at five, and that was it. Things don't work that way any longer.

"Our employees and distributors have the flexibility to do things that are important to them. They can go to their kids' programs when they need to. We have one couple who are both senior executives at Amway. They moved their child to a private school near the office so she can still go to school for recess duty because it is important to her."

When asked about his formula for success, DeVos says that "Creativity—the ability to think outside the box, to see things beyond the vision of others—is a key element." But you must also be able to communicate your ideas, to engage others in your vision.

"None of us is able to be successful all alone," he said. "If we are going to achieve anything, we need to take others with us, and they aren't going to go along as hostages. They need to go along as enthusiastic volunteers.

"The third principle of success is persistence, not single-minded, blind pursuit, but persistence in the appropriate sense of not accepting no for an answer. No product is perfect for everyone, but if you really believe that what you are offering is important and the individual is going to benefit from your product and your service, you have a responsibility to offer it to them. Accepting it or not becomes their choice.

"It is also important to continually seek ways to improve what we do. There is no one perfect idea. Each one can be refined and shaped. When we fully understand the core value of our idea, we can more easily execute all of the elements to get the right mix that will ensure the highest probability of success."

—— POSITIVE ACTION STEPS ——

☞ The three As of success are action, attitude, and atmosphere. Strive to keep all three positive.

☞ Allow others to decide what is best for them.

☞ Reinforce your positive attitude by reading positive articles and listening to motivational tapes.

DAY 89

STREET KID TO BRAIN SURGEON: BEN CARSON

G o down to the fish market and look in the crab barrel. They never have to put a lid on it because if one crab starts to crawl out, the others will grab him and pull him back down. That's what negative peer pressure does."

The speaker is Dr. Benjamin Carson, the forty-two-year-old director of pediatric neurosurgery at the prestigious Johns Hopkins University and Hospital. He peppers his talk to one of the hundreds of youth groups he regularly addresses with stories of how he made it from the mean streets of Detroit to his position today as one of America's most respected neurosurgeons.

Raised by a mother with a third-grade education, he overcame grinding poverty and a pathological temper that once drove him to attempt to stab a friend in a dispute over which station to listen to on a transistor radio.

The blade of the cheap camping knife snapped when it hit the other boy's belt buckle, saving young Carson from prison or worse. "The other boy fled in terror," Dr. Carson said, "but at that moment, I was more horrified than he was, because I suddenly realized that I had tried to kill someone—over nothing.

"I raced home; locked myself in the bathroom and started thinking. Over the next three hours, I concluded that one of the reasons I got angry was because I always had to be the center of attention. I realized that if you don't allow yourself to become angry, others cannot get the upper hand with you. No external influence can do that to me any longer. I have power over it."

Dr. Carson believes that the secret desire of most young people is to find what Ralph Waldo Emerson labeled "the chief want of young lives: to find someone who will make us do what we can." His mother provided that influence in his own life.

Despite the fact that she was uneducated and suffered frequent bouts of severe depression, she had high expectations for her sons. "She was my Emerson," Dr. Carson said. "She demanded that I do all I could. She required me and my brother to read two books a week and give her a report on them."

Books opened a whole new world to young Carson. Knowledge became his escape and allowed him to transform himself from the one others regarded as the class dummy into the smartest kid in the fifth grade.

He graduated at the top of his class at Detroit's Southwestern High School and was recruited by a number of leading universities, but his options were limited. All required a $10 fee to take the entrance exam; he had only one ten dollar bill. He could apply to only one college. He chose Yale and won a ninety percent academic scholarship.

Plagued by money problems and insecurity, near the end of the first semester, he was failing in chemistry and overcome by self-doubt. *What am I doing at Yale anyway?* he asked himself. *Who do I think I am? Just a dumb Black kid from the poor side of Detroit who has no business trying to make it through Yale with all these intelligent, affluent students.*

As he considered his options, Carson realized that business or teaching held little appeal for him. He had always wanted to be a doctor, and the opportunity was slipping from his grasp.

His only hope was to score well on the final exam in chemistry. As he crammed for the test, he knew it was hopeless. He was simply too far behind. He fell exhausted into bed and whispered a prayer: "God, I'm sorry. Please forgive me for failing You and for failing myself."

As he slept, he dreamed that he was the only person in the chemistry lecture hall, watching as an odd ethereal figure worked chemistry problems on the blackboard. When he awoke, Carson vividly remembered the problems and quickly wrote them down before they faded from memory.

He knew enough about psychology to assume that his subconscious was attempting to work out unresolved problems, but what followed could be explained only as miraculous. When the professor handed out the test booklet, it contained the exact problems the shadowy figure had solved in his dream. When the final chemistry grades were posted, Mr. Carson had scored ninety-seven percent.

From that day forward, he had no doubt that he was on the right path, that great things were going to happen in his life, and he had better be ready for them. He graduated from Yale University and the University of Michigan Medical School and completed his internship and advanced surgical training at Johns Hopkins. After a year at a neurosurgery post in Western Australia, he returned to Johns Hopkins where he was named assistant professor of neurological surgery and director of pediatric neurosurgery.

Today, Dr. Carson works miracles in the lives of others, often accepting cases considered hopeless. He gained worldwide recognition in 1987 for his role as the primary surgeon in a successful operation to separate Siamese twins joined at the back of the head. Five months in planning and twenty-two hours in execution, the surgery marked the first time such an operation was performed with both twins surviving.

The soft-spoken surgeon has pioneered a number of medical techniques, earning him the respect of the medical community and the eternal gratitude of his patients and their parents. He holds eight honorary doctorates, he has written scores of technical articles, he is the subject of numerous articles and interviews, and there is a movie and television show based on his life in the works.

Asked when it's all over for Dr. Ben Carson how he would like to be remembered, he replied simply: "He used his God-given talents to try to make a better life for himself and everyone around him."

—— POSITIVE ACTION STEPS ——

☞ Avoid others who find it easier to keep you down instead of lifting themselves up.

☞ You can overcome even the worst circumstances with hard work and faith.

☞ Believe in yourself and everything is possible. Doubt yourself and nothing is possible.

DAY 90

THINKING BIG:
JIM VIGUE

Jim Vigue doesn't think big—he thinks enormous.

The president of Waterville, Maine-based Firstmark Corporation, a venture capital and financial services consulting firm, the forty-three-year-old Vigue said, "Someone once told me, 'Your biggest fault is that you don't think big enough.' Since then, I've tried to stretch myself, to do more, to think bigger."

The Maine native also capitalizes on his home state's reputation for hard work and reticence. Although he counts numerous famous personalities among his clients, he won't name names, not even for reference checks. "If a new client asks for a client list to check out our service, we have to refuse," he said. "We absolutely protect the confidentiality of our relationships.

"Our philosophy is: If we take care of clients first, the business will take care of itself. Most people in our business think mostly about commissions or fees they'll generate, but we don't look at it that way. We look at how we can help our clients, how we can solve their problems and address their concerns."

Integrity has paid off for Vigue. In an industry characterized by spectacular ethical lapses and persistent client turnover, he hasn't lost a managed client in more than twenty years, and taking care of clients has taken care of the bottom line. The firm's market value is in excess of $10 million, managed assets are in the hundred millions, and Firstmark's financial services business was up fifty percent last year.

Vigue showed a definite entrepreneurial bent early in his career. As a college student, he ran his own hot dog concession and invested a portion of the cash the business generated. Upon graduation from Colby College in 1972, Vigue earned his securities license and accepted a position with a local investment firm. A short stint as a partner in another investment firm followed before Vigue started his own investment advisory firm. He later merged with a small New York publicly owned consulting company to form Firstmark.

Vigue credits much of his success to following the success principles of authors like Napoleon Hill. "But," he says, "if you think you are going to read the book and everything is going to happen automatically, you are going to be disappointed. That's where persistence comes in. A lot of people will try something once and if they fail, they will never try it again. Our philosophy is that we will try something and if it doesn't work, we are just that much closer next time."

Vigue also believes the Master-Mind concept is vitally important. "It's almost impossible to build anything of substance without having good people working with you," he said. "It starts with your spouse; if you don't have a strong, proactive, supportive spouse, it will be very difficult to achieve great success. Then you go from there to bring in key people.

"Specialized knowledge is also critical in our business," Vigue said. "We have to have to offer something the competition doesn't. We've built our firm by having a number of generalists and a lot of people who really specialize. We meet every week to make sure we integrate our corporate and individual goals through the use of the Master-Mind alliance."

Vigue has built strong client relationships by going the extra mile for clients and is currently writing a book (his second) on servicing the rich and famous. "It's a concentrated, personalized approach to marketing by going the extra mile to find out what interests people and getting involved in their lives," he said.

"We basically try to help people, then let the business take care of itself. If there is an opportunity, there is; if there isn't, there isn't. I've been friends with people for years, sometimes, before we've done any business.

"In the end, though, if you want to do business with highly successful people, you have to have some substance. Our clients know we are going to be here tomorrow. Our integrity and track record speak for themselves.

"We also like to think that out here in Maine we see things a little differently. We're not tied to the Wall Street rumor mill. Because the sun rises first in the state of Maine, we see things a little more clearly," Vigue said.

—— POSITIVE ACTION STEPS ——

☞ To do business with people of substance you must become a person of substance.

☞ When you concentrate on helping people, business will follow.

☞ Demonstrate you are worthy of others' trust before you ask them to trust you with their money.

CHAPTER FOURTEEN

PUTTING IT ALL TOGETHER

O ver the past ninety days, you have been exposed to many success tips, methods, and techniques. You may have noticed along the way that many of them seem to be closely related to each other. Indeed, they are. The individual ideas and principles add up to a philosophy of personal achievement composed of five general categories:

1. **Goal setting**. Without a definite goal, you will just drift with the current. Know where you are going and how you are going to get there. Use whatever method works best for you to set your specific goals and follow through with action to accomplish them.

2. **Maintain a positive mental attitude**. If you think you can accomplish something, you have a very good chance of doing it. If you believe that you will fail, you already have. A positive mental attitude is, therefore, the starting point of all success. There are many strategies for developing a positive attitude and remaining positive in the face of minor setbacks. Whichever technique works best for you, the important thing to remember is that you can do it—if you think you can.

3. **Never stop learning**. Knowledge is indeed power—the power to grow and develop, the power to react to changing times, the power to seize opportunities in emerging trends. By continuing to read and learn about the world around you, you prepare yourself not only to react positively to life but also to take the actions necessary to create the life you desire for yourself and your family.

4. **Develop a pleasing personality based on good character**. Most of us need the cooperation of partners, co-workers, friends, relatives, and even strangers to achieve great success. You have read about many techniques for developing a pleasing personality built on solid character. As you apply the techniques you've learned, others will begin to respond more favorably to you. Doors that once seemed to be closed will suddenly open to you. You will find that others will cheerfully work with you to help you achieve your goals.

5. **Trust in yourself and your mind to achieve any goal**. The mind is a wonderful thing. When you commit to a goal or idea,

your subconscious mind will immediately set out to make it a reality. There are many methods for keeping a thought fixed firmly in mind, but the important thing is to believe in your ability to make it happen. As Napoleon Hill said, "What the mind can conceive and believe, it can achieve." Dream big. Your subconscious will act on a big goal just as readily as it will a small one. Reach for the stars.

You now have the tools to achieve any goal you set your mind to. Set your goals and get into action—now. If from time to time you need a little motivational lift, simply re-read a few appropriate pages from this book. Even better, teach others some of the techniques and secrets you have learned over the past ninety days. Nothing clarifies your own thinking more than teaching something to others. And nothing helps further your success as much as helping others succeed.

KEY POSITIVE ACTION STEPS SUMMARY
Positive Attitude:

1. Maintain a positive mental attitude.

2. Associate with positive people. Avoid doomsayers.

3. Engage in positive conversations. Avoid complaining.

4. Keep motivated by reading positive, motivational materials.

5. Visualize the worst-case scenario. Often you'll find you can live with the worst case, and you can take comfort in the fact that the worst case almost never happens anyway.

6.   Fix problems, don't fix blame.

7.   When you face a difficult decision, sleep on it.

8.   Realize that you can do just about anything—if you believe you can.

9.   Make it a habit to go the extra mile.

10. Focus on solutions, not on problems.

Developing a Positive Personality:

1.   Always do more than you're asked to do.

2.   Find something that needs to be done and do it.

3.   Take a genuine interest in co-workers and customers.

4.   Learn to listen at least as much as you talk.

5.   Treat others the way you would want to be treated.

6.   Don't wait for others to ask for help; establish goodwill by looking for ways to help them now.

7.   Never threaten anyone. It may come back to haunt you.

8.   Break bad habits by replacing them with good habits.

9.   Always be sincere. And always be willing to prove you're sincere in your goals.

Knowledge and Learning:

1. Write out a plan for achieving your goal. Break it down into short-, medium-, and long-range goals.

2. Never be rushed into a decision. If you can't have time to think about it, forget it.

3. Spend a few minutes three times a day envisioning yourself achieving your ultimate goal (i.e. wealth, new car, etc.).

4. Realize that it is not too late to change the direction of your life.

5. View defeat as merely a learning process.

6. Keep motivated by reading positive motivational materials.

7. Sticking with your goal until you achieve it will teach you the determination and focus to achieve all your future goals.

8. Stop fighting change. Instead, explore ways to take advantage of it.

Teamwork:

1. Motivate with rewards for good service.

2. Call an old colleague and catch up with what's new. Renewing ties strengthens your network.

3. Compliment co-workers on their achievements.

4. Share the credit with co-workers.

5. Learn to delegate. Ask for recommendations instead of solving problems for your employees. Let them learn and grow.

6. Find out how what you do fits in with the rest of the organization.

7. Treat everyone in the company, those below you as well as those above, with common courtesy.

8. Try to help at least one person a day. Start today.

9. Two people working together can achieve far more than they can working separately.

10. Seek a partner who is strong in those areas where you are weak.

The Power of the Mind:

1. Post pictures of your goal where you will see them every day.

2. Spend at least a half hour every day to read, study, and reflect.

3. Use quiet time to focus on solutions to problems and setbacks.

4. Write down the bad habits you want to replace, and next to them write the good habits you will use to replace them.

5. Let daydreams point the way to what you want most in life.

6. Trust that there are forces in the universe we don't understand, but that if we work for good, we will attract good things.

7. Try using positive affirmations like "I can do it" repeated over and over to relax you into a meditative state.

8. Develop a definiteness of purpose—a goal you fix in your mind until it is reached.

Organization:

1. Organize your day to reduce stress.

2. Set aside a half hour each day for creative thinking.

3. Set aside ten percent of earnings for savings and investment.

4. Strive for balance. Work, study, and reflecting are all important components of success.

5. Adopt the motivator "Do It Now" to avoid procrastination.

Business:

1. Set up a work schedule and stick with it.

2. Make "to do" lists of what you need to accomplish to further your success—and set about doing it.

3. Don't "sell" prospects. Focus on solving their problems.

4. Build a relationship first. Sales will come later.

5. Do profitable tasks as long as you have the time—attend to details later.

6. Keep records of your activities to find the most profitable times to perform each task.

7. Deal with others as if your reputation were on the line—it is.

8. Keep in touch with what's going on by talking to your employees, co-workers, and customers.

9. Recognize, relate, assimilate, and apply the information that is readily available all round you.

10. When conditions change, don't assume you know why. Ask employees and customers.

Enthusiasm:

1. To be enthusiastic, act enthusiastic.

2. Associate with positive enthusiastic people. Enthusiasm is contagious.

3. Take a genuine interest in those around you.

4. Defeat is temporary if your commitment is permanent.

5. When faced with adversity, remember those who have overcome even greater obstacles and succeeded.

ABOUT THE AUTHOR

Don Green, a resident of Wise, Virginia, the birthplace of Napoleon Hill, brings nearly forty-five years of banking, finance, and entrepreneurship experience to his role as executive director of the Napoleon Hill Foundation. Since 2000, he has traveled worldwide and used his finance skills to grow the Foundation's funds in order to continue the Foundation's educational outreach.

Don Green has both modeled leadership skills as a CEO and taught them through the PMA (Positive Mental Attitude) Science of Success course at the University of Virginia's College at Wise. Don specializes in discussing his personal experiences in leadership and providing audiences with proven methods of applying Dr. Hill's success philosophy to business and life.

THANK YOU FOR READING THIS BOOK!

If you found any of the information helpful, please take a few minutes and leave a review on the bookselling platform of your choice.

BONUS GIFT!

Don't forget to sign up to try our newsletter and grab your free personal development ebook here:

soundwisdom.com/classics

Because Your Success Matters